# DEDICATION

To Amy, my beautiful wife.
She is God's greatest gift for me

# Moments
## of Ministry
### Dan Lynch

### PUBLISHED by PARABLES
*Earthly Stories with a Heavenly Meaning*

Moments of Ministry

Copyright ©Dan Lynch
December, 2017

*Published By Parables*
December, 2017

THE HOLY BIBLE, NEW INTERNATIONAL VERSION®, NIV® Copyright © 1973, 1978, 1984, 2011 by Biblica, Inc.® Used by permission. All rights reserved worldwide.

    ISBN 978-1-945698-42-2
    Printed in the United States of America

Readers should be aware that Internet Web sites offered as citations and/or sources for further information may have been changed or disappeared between the time this was written.

# Moments of Ministry
## Dan Lynch

PUBLISHED by PARABLES
*Earthly Stories with a Heavenly Meaning*

# About the Author

Dan Lynch was born in Butte Montana in 1938 and during World War 2 he moved to San Francisco California. Dan was brought up in an Irish ethnic neighborhood and attended Catholic school for six years. He then went to public school where he played several sports and made All City in two different sports. He met his beautiful bride, Amy Maxine, and began dating her in high school. Dan enlisted in the Navy and served aboard the USS Missouri. In 1957, during Dan's Navy days, He and Amy Maxine married. Dan had several jobs before finally becoming a San Francisco Police Officer in 1962. He stayed with the department until he retired on a disability pension in 1978.

In 1978 they moved to Idaho where Dan could hunt and fish his life away, but was called by God at a Billy Graham Crusade. Dan decided to go back to school where he received his theological degree and became a pastor and teacher. He attended San Francisco City College, San Francisco State University, Golden Gate Law School and after he came to the Lord he went to Inland Empire School of the Bible and Northwest Theological School. where he received his theological degree and became a pastor and teacher. He attended San Francisco City College, San Francisco State University, Golden Gate Law School and after he came to the Lord he went to Inland Empire School of the Bible and Northwest Theological School.

Dan has since retired where he spent 51 years as a Police Officer, Chaplain of Jail, Chaplain of Sheriff and a Chaplain of Local and State Police and Pastor. He has taught at Moody Bible College and has also been a teaching Pastor at his present church since 2000.

He plays golf at every opportunity and his best buddy is John L. Sullivan, his dog, who is a Boxer.

Dan has been married to his beautiful wife for 58 years and they have two daughters, Dannell and Colleen and two grandchildren, Josh and Amy.

# January 1

Criminals can be really stupid, and I think I have met one of the stupidest of all. This guy came into a convenience store to rob it but the clerk was very busy with customers. He waited and after a while filled out a chance to win a trip to the super bowl. He finally robbed the store and the clerk remembered that he had filled out the ticket. We had a brilliant idea and put up a poster saying he had won and had to come in at a certain time to collect his winning ticket. He showed up and we arrested him. He was very angry and threatened to sue us for not giving him the super bowl ticket. We all have a winning ticket to give to everyone that is a ticket to heaven.

Matthew 28:19
Therefore go and make disciples of all nations, baptizing them in the name of the Father and of the Son and of the Holy Spirit, and teaching them to obey everything I have commanded you.

Dan Says:
"This is the year I will share my faith with others."

# MOMENTS OF MINISTRY

# January 2

"How many pairs does that make now?" I would always ask the eye doctor when he came to the mission. He said, "a lot". He would come to the mission and there was one man who lost his glasses every time. We tried every possible way to keep him from losing his glasses, we tried those strings that hung around your neck, and we even tried rubber bands, but he always lost them. I asked the Doc, "How many pairs of glasses are you going to give him?" His answer was: "I will provide him with glasses as long as he needs them". I guess that Doc knew what it was to be a giver.

Matthew 6:2
So when you give to the needy, do not announce it with trumpets, as the hypocrites do in the synagogues and on the streets, to be honored by others. Truly I tell you, they have received their reward in full.

Dan Says:
"When it comes to giving, some people stop at nothing."

# MOMENTS OF MINISTRY

# January 3

It does not matter if you are undercover or not, when a cop hears a police car with the siren going he just has to go to the curb and watch. They were approaching at high speed; it was an unmarked car after some men in a Chevy. As they slowed to make the corner, one of them leaned out the window and threw me a package. I watched as they got pulled over and taken into custody. They were going to Park Station, so I headed there myself. Everyone at the station knew. I would not be challenged as I approached the narcotics officers. I said to the suspects, "You guys lost this package when you went around that corner", and put the kilo of grass on the table. All the cops went along with the gag and it was one funny scene. Even when they went to court they refused to believe I was a cop.

Romans 10:14
How, then, can they call on the one they have not believed in? And how can they believe in the one of whom they have not heard?

Dan Says:
"We only really believe as much of the Bible as we practice."

# MOMENTS OF MINISTRY

# January 4

I was standing on the quarterdeck with the officer of the day. We were waiting for the sailors to return to ship from shore leave. Sometimes I was needed to help guys get to their bunk. The officer of the day was a good guy and did not try to put us on report if they had a little too much to drink. Up the gangplank came Jerry, a third class petty officer, who had many years in the service, and he had a bottle of booze in each hand. The officer said to Jerry, "I am going to turn my back and I want to hear two splashes and then you get to bed." Sure enough, he heard two splashes and as I turned to look, there went Jerry with the two bottles and no shoes.

Matthew 10:26
So do not be afraid of them, for there is nothing concealed that will not be disclosed, or hidden that will not be made known.

Dan Says:
"The easiest person you can deceive is yourself."

# MOMENTS OF MINISTRY

# January 5

When I was selected for the K-9 unit for the police department, I learned the first thing I had to do was select and train my dog. Both the dog and I went through training at the same time and we developed an understanding of each other. The dog, in order to please me, always had to obey every command I gave him. Soon I began to read my dog and to see if he was really working as he was supposed to or just going through the motions. I have observed my dog during a building search walk back and forth like he was really working and then step right over a burglar's legs. You see, he was just going through the motions to make me happy. I wonder if we do the same thing with God and just go through the motions.

John 14:15
If you love me, keep my commands.

Dan Says:
"If you do not obey fully, you are disobedient."

# Moments
## of Ministry

# January 6

I used to fish with a man who lived up the street from me. He was a great fisherman and I learned a lot from him. He and I spent a lot of time fishing and tying flies together. As we spent more and more time together, I began to witness to him and tell him of our Lord. He always just brushed me off and said that he was not interested right now. He did, however, have one really bad habit: when he was frustrated, he would take the Lord's name in vain. Finally, I had enough; one day while fishing he screamed, "Jesus Christ" and I went to him and said, "You are always calling Him, now I am going to introduce you to Him." After I went into great detail about my relationship with Jesus he did not say a word. He never spoke to me again and I do not know what happened to him, as he eventually moved away. But this I do know, I did my part.

Philippians 2:9-10
Therefore God exalted him to the highest place and gave him the name that is above every name, that at the name of Jesus every knee should bow, in heaven and on earth and under the earth.

Dan Says:
"Remember it is with our mouth that we witness to others."

# Moments of Ministry

# January 7

He had accepted the Lord while he was in jail and now he was out, looking for work. He was a carpet layer by trade and my wife and I decided to hire him to do some work for us. Our kitchen had carpet in it and my wife did not like it, so we decided to have him put in linoleum. He came to the house and stripped the carpet out and asked for money to buy the materials he needed to finish the job. We gave him the money and that was the last we saw of him. After about two weeks, we decided that we had been had. Just as we were going to get someone else, he pulled up in the driveway and came in to finish the work. I asked him what had happened and he said" I was going to rip you off, but God would not let me." God does work in mysterious ways.

Matthew 10:16
I am sending you out like sheep among wolves. Therefore be as shrewd as snakes and as innocent as doves.

Dan Says:
"If you want the best place to place your trust, place it in Jesus."

# MOMENTS OF MINISTRY

# January 8

While I was still in Bible College, I was offered the opportunity to assist one of my professors in his church. I became his assistant and in the course of time, he was offered another position, which he accepted. The church then decided to keep me as the pastor and so I got another student to come and help me. We had a lot of fun together and as we learned something in school, we would put it into practice at our church. In spite of our inexperience, the church continued to grow. One Sunday, I asked Bob, my helper, to take charge of the part of the service that included the collection. He stood in front of the congregation and said "Now reach in the pocket of the guy in front of you and give like you always wanted to". I know that Jesus smiled at our efforts that day.

Colossians 3:23
Whatever you do, work at it with all your heart, as working for the Lord, not for human masters

Dan Says:
"If you are truly doing it for God, you cannot do it wrong."

# MOMENTS OF MINISTRY

# January 9

As soon as I came into the jail it started, everyone was telling me that Joe in "K" tank wanted to talk to me. I got to my office and asked the guard to bring Joe to me. Joe's smile lit up the whole room and I asked what was up. He said that he had led a guard to the Lord. He told me as he was discussing the Lord with the guard that the bars seem to have disappeared and the guard accepted Jesus. I told him I would talk to the guard and give him a Bible. When that guard came in, he was full of smiles. He said he accepted the Lord and was now a Christian. He told me as they were talking the bars seemed to disappear. Now I bet some of you do not believe that those bars did disappear, but this I know: nothing can get in God's way when He wants to do a work in someone's life.

Ephesians 3:7
I became a servant of this gospel by the gift of God's grace given me through the working of his power.

Dan Says:
"Anyone can become a working servant of The Most High."

# MOMENTS OF MINISTRY

# January 10

We had a tutor who was teaching my wife and I Hebrew. He had a wonderful little trick to teach us numbers. Several times during our sessions he would ask us what time it was in Hebrew. We soon learned to hate the words "Ma haShaha?" or "What time is it?" We would have to start at one in our head and count forward until we reached the right time. He knew I dreaded the question and got pleasure watching me. Once, while we were visiting Israel, a woman came up to me and asked, you guessed it, "What time is it?" As soon as she left my wife said to me "boy did you ever give her a dirty look". I knew what she said was true and I was sorry. See how an innocent habit can hurt others; watch what habits you develop.

1 Timothy 5:13
Besides, they get into the habit of being idle and going about from house to house.

Dan Says:
"It is a lot easier to make habits than to break habits."

# MOMENTS OF MINISTRY

# January 11

I love to play golf; however, I am not very good at the game. I was in heaven when I got the opportunity to go on staff at a church where the pastor was a retired golf professional. We developed a good relationship and soon would play golf on our off days. He would always beat me by a wide margin. One time, at a men's retreat in Montana, we were playing field golf. That's where they mow a field and put out pie tins with a stake through them. I was actually winning and we only had two holes to go. As I lined up for my next shot, I felt something on my foot. I looked down and there was a snake. Well my game went to pot and the pastor won easily. That snake was my downfall, but the Word says there is another snake that will be the downfall of many.

Revelation 12:9
The great dragon was hurled down - that ancient serpent called the devil, or Satan, who leads the whole world astray.

Dan Says:
"I never met a snake that I liked, so I do not hang around snake places."

# Moments
## of Ministry

# January 12

Have you ever watched a group of young children get together and make a collective decision? First, one will say, we should do this, and they all agree, until another says we should do that. Then they will split along some sort of lines, boy against the girls, etc. After much discussion, they review their options and then listen to the loudest one (Kind of the "squeaky wheel" syndrome.). Some people never get beyond that type of decision-making. The Word of God gives us a system to help us make the right decision. We should ask wise counsel from Godly men and then pray for guidance. I bet that God does not answer the loudest prayer as fast as He answers the fervent prayer of a righteous man.

Philippians 4:6
Do not be anxious about anything, but in every situation, by prayer and petition, with thanksgiving, present your requests to God.

Dan Says:
"A prayer that is whispered may cause God to listen harder."

# Moments of Ministry

# January 13

The city required us to go on to a sewer from our old septic system. We had a crew come out to do the work; I never realized how much work was involved. They came with big machines and had to remove four fences and lots of plants. In fact, we lost two large trees that I had planted years ago. I was not very happy with the way the yard was looking, but a landscaper friend of mine came by and told me not to worry, in a month the snow will fall and my yard will look like everyone else's. Kind of like how Christ covered our sin so we would look like everyone else.

Isaiah 1:18
Though your sins are like scarlet, they shall be as white as snow; though they are red as crimson, they shall be like wool.

Dan Says:
"We can be sure of the grace Jesus has given us regarding our sins."

# MOMENTS OF MINISTRY

## January 14

My daughter was working at a flower stand. She had to go to an appointment and she left my wife and me to watch the stand. Right after she left, a lady came up and wanted some flowers. My wife and I had no idea what they looked like, so the lady pointed them out for us. I looked on the price sheet and could not find that flower, so I said, "two bucks". That sounded reasonable to me for a bunch of flowers, so we just began to charge everyone two dollars. We did a rousing business that day as the word spread. When my daughter got back to the stand, she was not very happy with us. We sure made a lot of other people happy though!

Isaiah 35:1-2
The desert and the parched land will be glad; the wilderness will rejoice and blossom. Like the crocus, 2 it will burst into bloom; it will rejoice greatly and shout for joy. The glory of Lebanon will be given to it, the splendor of Carmel and Sharon; they will see the glory of the Lord, the splendor of our God.

Dan Says:
"Do not give joy at someone else's expense."

# MOMENTS
## OF MINISTRY

## January 15

It was dark in there and they had a weapon. I was not about to turn on my flashlight and give them a target. I had heard shots and determined they came from another floor of the department store we were searching. As I came around a corner, I saw a man with a gun so I opened fire. Imagine my surprise when the man disappeared in a shower of glass. I had just shot a mirror. I did take a lot of ribbing about that incident. Later, one of the old timers asked me if I would partner up with him. When I asked why, he said, "To me, fear is what gets a good cop and his partner home every night."

Proverbs 1:7
The fear of the Lord is the beginning of knowledge, but fools despise wisdom and instruction.

Dan Says:
"A healthy fear of God can give you an enjoyable life."

# Moments of Ministry

# January 16

When I was young, we did not have newspaper racks. We had vendors who stood on the corner. I used to love to listen to Chester yell what the headlines were, even before I could read. I remember thinking that Chester was the smartest man I ever knew. He could tell you the statistics on any ball player or team. It was not until I was around twelve or so that I realized that Chester was mentally retarded. After I found out, Chester became even more special.

1 Samuel 16:7
The Lord does not look at the things people look at. People look at the outward appearance, but the Lord looks at the heart.

Dan Says:
"What is special to God is not always as special to us."

# Moments of Ministry

# January 17

I am truly married to an angel. I am the type of husband that would drive an ordinary woman crazy. I have this habit of collecting people, kind of like how some people collect stray dogs. They do not follow me home, but I bring them. Some of them stay a few days and others, a few years. I remember one day driving into the driveway with a man in my car. When she saw us she asked me "is he here for dinner or to stay with us?" As it turned out he did stay with us for several years, but then he went out on his own. They all end up calling Maxine "Mom" and she does care for them like a mother. When they do move on, they make Mom's prayer list and are never forgotten.

Proverbs 12:4
A wife of noble character is her husband's crown.

Dan Says:
"A good wife will put up with all our silly ideas to help us succeed."

# Moments of Ministry

# January 18

Standing in the water up to our waists, the snow falling, it was March and I was about to baptize my future son-in-law. He had accepted Christ as his savior and wanted to be baptized immediately. His commitment to the Lord was evident and he has never lost his desire to serve Him. He was a baggage handler at the airport and he went back to work and started a Bible study. He is still growing in the Lord and loves Him. I think one of the reasons for this is the commitment that my wife and I had to pray for godly men to marry our daughters. Both Colleen, and her sister, Dannell, married fine Christian men and are walking close to the Lord.

>Colossians 4:2
>Devote yourselves to prayer, being watchful and thankful.

Dan Says:
"We cannot pray too much for our children."

# MOMENTS OF MINISTRY

# January 19

The call from one of my mentors left me surprised; Pastor Mort called to ask me to take his class at the Bible College. I was confused, as I knew it was his favorite class: teaching freshmen how to study the Bible. I asked why he wanted me to teach this term and he explained that he had been diagnosed with a brain tumor and did not think he could do as good a job as he wanted. I agreed and always tried to transmit to the students the love that Mort did. It was so wonderful to watch those students make great discoveries for themselves and become excited about the Word. That class changed the way I teach and in about a hundred years I may be able to teach like Pastor Mort.

Proverbs 17:17
A friend loves at all times.

Dan Says:
"You really never lose good friends; they are part of who you are."

# Moments
## of Ministry

# January 20

I can finally, after seventy years, stand the taste of maple. When I was a small child in Montana, my mom had a cupboard and in it she stored a lot of our food. One of the things that she stored was maple sugar. It was hard to get during the Second World War. Well one day, I got into it and ate about a ton, boy was I ever sick. Now after all these years, I still have a reaction to the smell and taste of maple. I guess that I ate way too much of a good thing. Funny how we can get caught into something that seems so good, but in the end it only makes you sick. I can tell you one thing that you can never get enough of, the Word of God.

Romans 8:28
And we know that in all things God works for the good of those who love him, who have been called according to his purpose.

Dan Says:
"Too much of even a good thing can be bad for you."

# Moments
## of Ministry

# January 21

The sea was tossing us like a piece of driftwood; we had gone down to San Diego to pick up a destroyer escort that had been in mothballs for several years. There was an ocean going tug that two ships in tow. We were on the boat in the rear. Soon, we hit a terrific Pacific storm and the towline parted. We used the radio to ask the tug to come get us, but they said they could not as it was too stormy. We put out a life raft and it sunk and never came up again, we then threw over a lifejacket and it also sank. We were heading for the cliffs of Morro Bay when we saw a seaplane. Thinking we would be rescued, we were very happy. But the plane was taking pictures for the evening news. All of a sudden, there came an old LST (Landing Ship, Tank) and we were saved. The conversion of that old ship was not easy, but neither are some of the conversions we are supposed to do.

Joshua 1:9
Be strong and courageous. Do not be afraid; do not be discouraged, for the Lord your God will be with you wherever you go.

Dan Says:
"The help that the Lord sends is not always in the form we would like."

# Moments of Ministry

# January 22

The nickel came sliding down the lane, when I saw it I simply picked it up and threw it back to the bowler. When his friends saw how cheap he was, they really got on his case. Pretty soon, down the lane came a shiny silver dollar. It was customary to give a pinsetter at least a quarter. It was a good way to make a few bucks before the automatic pinsetters came into the lanes. We could really make it hard on someone if we set the pins a little off spot, or we could really make you look good by placing the pins closer together. If it was a money match you always set the pins straight. It was amazing that someone you cannot see can influence your performance. We cannot see the Lord, but He is always at work in our life.

Matthew 22:16
"Teacher," they said, "we know that you are a man of integrity and that you teach the way of God in accordance with the truth."

Dan Says:
"Check the unseen influences in your life."

# Moments
## of Ministry

# January 23

We lived on one of the steepest streets in San Francisco; it was so steep that the police motorcycle squad trained on it. We had a neighbor who was very pregnant and also had a small boy in a stroller when my wife was just going out to shop and stopped to chat. While they were talking, the stroller took off down the hill. My wife took off in hot pursuit and the little boy was holding on for all he was worth. His hair was standing straight up and his mouth was wide open, but there was no sound coming out. My wife was about one yard behind, when the stroller hit a tire on the sidewalk and bounced right into her hands. The neighbors eventually moved away from the city and about five years later they came to visit. That little boy was terrified of the hills. He did not know why, but we did. We all have fears without a known source and we have a perfect solution for all those fears.

> 1 John 4:18
> There is no fear in love. But perfect love drives out fear.

> Dan Says:
> "Fear can be good, if you are afraid of the evil in your life."

# MOMENTS OF MINISTRY

## January 24

On a plainclothes detail, walking down Market Street, I spotted a lump under the shirt of the man in front of us. I was sure that it was a gun hidden back there. We made a plan to capture the guy with no harm to us or any citizens. The plan was that I would go and get in front of the man and when I approached him, I would put him in a bear hug while my partner would grab the gun. Well I proceeded to get in front of him, and all of a sudden, I gave the guy a great big bear hug. Meanwhile, my partner reached under the shirt and then took off running in the opposite direction as fast as he could. When we finally got the whole thing sorted out, I learned that the lump was his pet snake. When my partner saw what he had, he took off. I know I would have done the same thing if it were I.

2 Corinthians 1:17
Was I fickle when I intended to do this? Or do I make my plans in a worldly manner so that in the same breath I say both "Yes, yes" and "No, no"?

Dan Says:
"Plans that are best made. Are those you pray about first?"

# MOMENTS
## OF MINISTRY

# January 25

I was very young when I got married and I was very happy. My wife Amy, and I lived off the base in a little cottage. Everyone was in the same boat as us, there was no jealously, as we were in the same circumstances. When we came home from the service, we found that all our friends had a jump start on their lives. We had to live with my wife's parents for a while and it was very hard on us. We finally got a small apartment in someone's basement. It was all ours and just us. We did not have a lot of material things, but we had a deep love for each other and a great hope for our future. I wish now that we had known the Lord then so we could have set priorities for ourselves, but God had His hands on us even then and we can look back and see how much He really loved us.

1 Peter 5:7
Cast all your anxiety on him because he cares for you.

Dan Says:
"Place yourselves in the hands of a loving God and enjoy his protection."

# Moments of Ministry

## January 26

My wife, granddaughter Amy, and I really enjoy watching the wild life in our yard. We have several feeders and a birdbath that give us a tremendous amount of entertainment all year long. We had some new neighbors move into the house next door, and guess what, they had a cat. This cat was a good hunter and every time we saw him with a bird or squirrel, we were heartbroken. I went next door and told the neighbors what was bothering us. They were really concerned and asked what they could do. I said, "If you put a bell on the cat it would warn the wildlife and solve the problem." We were out having coffee on the porch one morning when we heard this loud, "BONG! BONG! BONG!" And there was the cat, wearing a big old cowbell. Well that was a case of overkill, but we, as Christians, are like that to new believers, we put such a burden on them that they cannot live up to our expectations.

1 Corinthians 8:9
Be careful, however, that the exercise of your rights does not become a stumbling block to the weak.

Dan Says:
"Enjoy your freedom in Christ, so long as it does not imprison others."

# Moments of Ministry

# January 27

I am sure that you have run across people that say, "Now that I have accepted Christ into my life, my troubles are over." Not too long ago, I talked to a young man who said he no longer had to work, because his Christian brothers and sisters were supposed to take care of him. How foolish! Although we are supposed to take care of the needy, I see nowhere in scripture that we are to give aid to the lazy. Work was part of the curse that resulted from the fall of man in the garden. God said we would toil and reap what we sowed by the sweat of our brow. As followers of Christ, we are to be the best workers we can be. We have the world watching us. They may not know the Bible, but they know how we should act. God feeds the birds of the air, but He does not throw food in their nests. Paul said "All that you do, do for the glory of God", that includes work.

2 Thessalonians 3:10
For even when we were with you, we gave you this rule: "The one who is unwilling to work shall not eat."

Dan Says:
"A man should get his worth from his honest labor."

# Moments of Ministry

# January 28

I got a call from the fourth floor of the jail. A man wanted to talk to a chaplain. As I walked inside the unit, there was a man waiting for me, just inside the door. He asked if I was the chaplain he had read about in the newspaper, and I said that I was. He wanted to make sure he was talking to the chaplain that had a drinking problem in the past. I told him that was true and the Lord had given me the power to overcome that problem. I asked him if he wanted that power in his life and he said he would think about it. I went on with my work and about an hour later, I received a call to go back to his floor. Once again, he was waiting right inside the door. He stated that he wanted Christ in his life right now. The change was very dramatic in him. He worked harder at being a Christian than any other inmate I have ever seen. He came out of jail, went to school, and got a degree in counseling. I got a letter from him saying that he was a volunteer at his local jail and was showing others who had the power to set them free from the bondage of drugs and alcohol.

Colossians 1:13
For he has rescued us from the dominion of darkness and brought us into the kingdom of the Son he loves,

Dan Says:
"What a great delight is a life changed by God."

# Moments of Ministry

# January 29

There she was, walking down the road with an Uzi machine gun under her arm. She was holding out her thumb in the universal sign for hitch hiking, so we stopped and picked her up. She spoke some English, so we asked where she had been. She told us she had been at the front, up on the border. Hard to believe, but in Israel the soldier takes their private vehicles to war zones and sometimes, they even walk. They have been in a state of war for over sixty years. Everyone in the country, both men and women, serves for two years in the military and has reserve obligations for life, until the age of fifty-five. It is not too difficult to understand how they will be deceived by the man of peace spoken of in the Bible, but no real peace can come until Jesus comes as Messiah and is accepted by the Jews.

John 14:27
Peace I leave with you; my peace I give you. I do not give to you as the world gives. Do not let your hearts be troubled and do not be afraid.

Dan Says:
"Peace is not the absence of conflict, but the presence of God."

# MOMENTS
## OF MINISTRY

# January 30

While I was growing up, I never met any of my grandparents, so when I became a grandparent, I wanted to be unique. I came upon a plan and it was quite simple: I would keep about fifty toys in the trunk of my car and every time I saw my grandkids, I gave them a toy. Once, while I was on the way home, I spotted my daughter and grandkids walking down the road. I stopped to say hello and my little granddaughter, Amy, said to her playmate that was with her, "Just climb up here and get a toy." She never realized that this was not how every grandpa treated their grandkids. I knew I was spoiling them, but to this very day, they always smile when they see me coming. But the greatest gift that was given to them was by Jesus as he gave them salvation.

James 1:17
Every good and perfect gift is from above, coming down from the Father of the heavenly lights, who does not change like shifting shadows.

Dan Says:
"Pass on that great gift given to you to others, salvation"

# Moments of Ministry

# January 31

At the Federal Deposit Insurance Corporation, they train their employees to know counterfeit by teaching them to recognize the real thing. They never show them any counterfeit at all. When such a bill does come by, they recognize it at once because it just does not feel right. Maybe we should use that procedure in the church. We should always show our people the truth so that when a counterfeit comes to the door, or they hear it at school, they can tell the difference. There is a desire to want to know all about the enemy and that is good but only after they are grounded firmly in the truth. I believe that knowing the Word of God and caring for the lost can make us effective for Christ.

1 John 4:1
Dear friends, do not believe every spirit, but test the spirits to see whether they are from God, because many false prophets have gone out into the world.

Dan Says:
"Spend your time with the real thing, the Word of God."

# Moments of Ministry

# February 1

I was older than most when Jesus got a hold of me and the Lord had a lot of work to do in my life. I was a very argumentative type of person and was always known for my quick temper. While I was Chaplain at the jail, I ran into a man who truly hated me and was always disrupting my Bible studies. I finally had to have him locked in his cell while I worked in his section of the jail. When he left, I was happy and relieved to be rid of him. One day, as I was coming to work I ran into this man and he advanced on me ready to fight. I tried to just ignore him, but he came at me and threw a punch. His punch missed, but mine did not. I looked about to see if anyone had seen me knock him down and I thought I was in the clear. When I got to my office, I noticed the message light blinking. When I played the message it said, "Hello Slugger". I knew that word would spread rapidly about my temper.

Proverbs 16:32
Better a patient person than a warrior, one with self-control than one who takes a city.

Dan Says:
"You cannot get rid of your temper by losing it."

# MOMENTS
## OF MINISTRY

# February 2

Back in California, some years ago, I saw my favorite bumper sticker. The area where I lived was an affluent part of Marin County. Almost everyone had a lot of money. There were many movie stars and producers, as well as many other people who had large fortunes. I saw a pair of automobiles that were parked in a big circular driveway; either of the cars was worth more than several years of my annual salary. A woman appeared in a beautiful fur coat and had diamonds so big I could see them from the street. The best thing of all was a bumper sticker on her car, "TOO MUCH IS NOT ENOUGH." Well I guess that says it all. You can have it all here on earth and it will not be enough to get you into heaven. I really have it all right now. I have Jesus.

Matthew 6:21
For where your treasure is, there your heart will be also.

Dan Says:
"The problem with greed is you may get all you want."

# Moments of Ministry

# February 3

There, standing in my yard, is that beautiful golden pine tree; the only trouble is that it should be green. I had to call a tree removable specialist to drop it. If I had tried, I am sure it would have fallen on the roof of my neighbor. The man came and did a perfect job with no problems at all. Now there was a big hole in my yard and I missed that tree. You know it is kind of like the sin in our lives, we miss the pleasure and people, but we know our lives are better because it is gone. I have planted a beautiful olive tree in place of that pine, when we get rid of sin in our life I think Jesus replaces it with something beautiful.

Colossians 3:8
But now you must also rid yourselves of all such things as these: anger, rage, malice, slander, and filthy language from your lips.

Dan Says:
"The old computer science saying is true; 'Garbage in, Garbage Out'. We can replace garbage with scripture."

# Moments
## of Ministry

# February 4

Standing knee deep in the cool waters of the Little North Fork River, I had just hooked another fat cutthroat trout. I was fishing with a friend who was a much better fisherman than I. He came down to watch me land the struggling fish. This was my fifth fish and he had yet to get a single fish to rise to his fly. He asked me what I was using and I gave him some of my hand tied flies. He began to catch fish immediately. Isn't it funny how we are experts in our own little stream? You know I think that God places us in just the right place to become fishers of men also. Get to know the tools He has given you, read His Word and pray you will be able to harvest the fish in your pond.

Matthew 4:19
"Come, follow me," Jesus said, "and I will send you out to fish for people."

Dan Says:
"You catch more fish with knowledge than with luck."

# Moments of Ministry

# February 5

"Oh No!" I thought as the cell door slammed in the high security section of the jail. The alarm had sounded and there was no way the door would be opened soon. I looked over at the inmate and he was very scary. He looked like he had run a hundred yard dash in a ninety-yard gym. As we eyed each other, he asked what that was I was carrying. I told him it was my Bible and he said, "You are always welcome here, brother." You meet believers in the strangest places. That turned out to be one of the most pleasant hours I ever spent in the jail. Better watch out, that co-worker or neighbor you do not care for may be a brother or sister in the Lord.

2 Corinthians 13:14
May the grace of the Lord Jesus Christ, and the love of God, and the fellowship of the Holy Spirit be with you all.

Dan Says:
"When you accept Jesus Christ as your Savior you are never alone again."

# Moments
## of Ministry

# February 6

As I picked up my little Granddaughter, Amy, from pre-school I asked her what she had learned today. She showed me a paper that she had and then went on to tell me about some kittens and their mittens. The only thing was, as she read the story, she stated the mittens had lost their kittens. She had changed the story a little bit and it was true, but not written, as the author had intended. You know that is what some people do to the Word of God; they say what they want it to say in their words, not those of the author. The Bible is the written Word of God and is to be read as written. There is no need for other books or additional teaching to understand. The Bible can stand on its own just as the Holy Spirit gave it.

2 Timothy 3:16-17
All Scripture is God-breathed and is useful for teaching, rebuking, correcting and training in righteousness, so that the servant of God may be thoroughly equipped for every good work.

Dan Says:
"Change is good in a man, but not in the Word of God."

# Moments of Ministry

# February 7

I am one of those people that like to watch bowling on television. I am amazed at how consistent those men and women are when it comes to making the ball do exactly what they want it to do. Recently, I had the opportunity to watch a top-notch bowler practice. He was not trying to throw strike after strike; instead he was throwing at one pin over and over. I asked him why and he said, "To be good, you have to be committed to all parts of the game." It makes me wonder, as Christians, are we committed to doing all that the Lord told us to do? It would be great to be a fully committed Christian.

2 Timothy 2:15
Do your best to present yourself to God as one approved, a worker who does not need to be ashamed and who correctly handles the word of truth.

Dan Says:
"Consistency in the Word brings consistency in your life."

# Moments
## of Ministry

# February 8

When I think of Mike the Cop, I always have to smile. He had a way of doing things that was always just right. If you got into trouble, he would make the decision right on the spot whether to tell your Dad or not. More than once he would tell one of us that we just volunteered to do Mrs. Murphy's lawn or some other chore that needed doing. If you skipped school, you had better get out of the neighborhood, or he would catch you for sure. He was a man you could talk to and expect an honest answer. I never saw Mike arrest or shoot anyone; instead he was always helping them. I remember when Mike retired, he was not replaced with another cop, and instead they put on a radio car. If you asked the merchants and the kids, we wanted old Mike back. We liked that personal touch; you can still find it when you talk to God one on one.

Romans 13:4
For the one in authority is God's servant for your good. But if you do wrong, be afraid, for rulers do not bear the sword for no reason. They are God's servants, agents of wrath to bring punishment on the wrongdoer.

Dan Says:
"We obey man's law because we love God's Law."

# Moments
## of Ministry

# February 9

There I was, sitting in my office, talking to a man who wanted to be a volunteer in the jail religious program. He was relating to me how he was a changed man after serving a term in prison for a bank robbery. As we talked, he told me how he was arrested for a bank robbery in San Francisco, and suddenly I realized that I was one of the arresting officers. It is strange the way the Lord works. Here were two guys who were shooting at each other and now talking how God had changed our lives. We, as a team, did make some differences in the lives of some men in the jail as we gave our testimonies. I guess that God does have a good laugh at our expense once in awhile. This man used to say, "God can use you, even if you were a cop."

1 Corinthians 1:27
But God chose the foolish things of the world to shame the wise; God chose the weak things of the world to shame the strong.

Dan Says:
"Enemies can become brothers in Christ."

# Moments of Ministry

# February 10

Ever wear a mask to fool people? One time, while I was a police officer, a professional make up man came in to make up a few of us for undercover work. I knew he did a good job because my dog would not let me in the house when I got home that night. He would not let me get close enough for him to smell me so he would know me. You know fooling a dog and some crooks was easy, but I wonder if at times we put on Christian masks and try to fool God. You know the Word says He can read the tablets of our hearts and knows our very thoughts. Take some advice and put away your mask. Just be all that God wants you to be.

1 Thessalonians 2:5
You know we never used flattery, nor did we put on a mask to cover up greed - God is our witness.

Dan Says:
"Only a fool would try to fool God."

# Moments
## of Ministry

# February 11

During World War 2, everything was rationed: meat, gas, shoes, all kinds of food, and almost everything else. It was very hard to get some things and impossible to get others. In order to be fair, the government set up a system of stamps for almost everything. Soon people began trading stamps to get a needed item. We did not have a car, so we were able to trade gas stamps for meat stamps. One day, I decided to lick all our stamps and put them on the wall. I still remember the spanking I got for that stunt. When the government man came, he would not replace any stamps that were in excess of what we should have. All that trading and saving and I had lost it all. It is like saving good deeds to get into heaven, just do the good deeds because you love Jesus.

1 Timothy 6:9
Those who want to get rich fall into temptation and a trap and into many foolish and harmful desires that plunge people into ruin and destruction.

Dan Says:
"Watch out for what you want, you may get what you deserve."

# MOMENTS OF MINISTRY

# February 12

On the way to the coast to spend Thanksgiving with our daughter, we ran into a fierce snowstorm. I don't mind telling you, my prayer life suddenly improved. I asked the Lord for help and he sent me a truck. Now that may sound strange to you, but it made perfect sense to me. You see this truck had Alaska license plates and I figured that this guy knew how to drive in snow. Any time there was danger he would tap on the brakes several times to warn me. It was almost easy to drive with that truck to follow. You know it is like life, it is not always easy, but the Lord has sent us what we need to get through it. The Bible contains the wisdom of God Himself and is always at our disposal. So, next time you find yourself in one of life's storms, look to God to see what He has to say. He has said He will never leave us or forsake us.

James 5:13
Is anyone among you in trouble? Let them pray. Is anyone happy? Let them sing songs of praise.

Dan Says:
"When you follow God's directions you are never lost."

# Moments
## of Ministry

# February 13

We had just come down from the cellblocks and I was asking the pastor what he had thought of the man we had just visited. The man was a real miracle of God. He was as tough as you get and had spent many years in prison for murder and robbery. He was on his way out of the system and the Lord had used me to bring him into the kingdom. I was trying to find a church home for him. I asked the pastor what he thought and he said, "this man has to quit smoking before he can come into our body" I said that perhaps it would be better to get him to stop killing people first and work on the smoking later. You see, we must get our priorities straight. First get them to Christ and then let the Holy Spirit and His love change them. He can smoke and get to heaven; in fact he will probably get there before us.

2 Corinthians 5:17
Therefore, if anyone is in Christ, the new creation has come: The old has gone, the new is here!

Dan Says:
"Give a baby time to grow, even if he is older than you."

# MOMENTS OF MINISTRY

# February 14

As I looked at the beautiful blonde in the photograph, I knew she was the girl for me. I knew she was worth it, so I had my brother help me take the stupid cast off of my leg. She had said she would go to the dance with me and there was nothing going to keep me from going with her. In that photo, she was wearing shorts and had beautiful legs. I knew from that first look that she was for me. We had several dates and then she became my girl. Well it must have worked out, here we are fifty-seven years later, still together and I can say I love her more now than then. But you know, my love for Christ is even greater, as her love for Christ is also. If Jesus is not the center of your marriage put Him there now.

2 John 1:3
Grace, mercy and peace from God the Father and from Jesus Christ, the Father's Son, will be with us in truth and love.

Dan Says:
"It is easier to love through Jesus than to fight through Him. Put Him in the center of your marriage."

# Moments of Ministry

# February 15

Sitting on the porch during the warm summer days is really relaxing. The sound of the wind in the trees is like nothing else. I know that the name for the Holy Spirit in both the Old and New Testaments is the same word used for wind. You know that it is there, but you cannot see it. You see the effects of the wind and yet it is totally in its own control. The Old Testament uses the word Ruah, which is an unseen force that is always there. In the New Testament it is Pneuma and has the same meaning. The wind is uncontrollable, powerful, helpful, calming and also wild and destructive. It is a mystery of God we cannot solve, but we do know about the Holy Spirit. The effects of the wind can be controlled by use of a sail or windmill. And the Holy Spirit will also help us upon our request in earnest prayer.

Luke 11:13
If you then, though you are evil, know how to give good gifts to your children, how much more will your Father in heaven give the Holy Spirit to those who ask him!

Dan Says:
"Do not ask for the power of God unless you intend to use it."

# MOMENTS
## OF MINISTRY

# February 16

I guess I was in trouble again, as I drew the position of the back of the Paddy Wagon. The wagon was used to transport subjects to the jail after an arrest was made. As my police district was the tenderloin, where there was an abundance of winos and a low class of criminals, it was the worst duty you could draw. Well, we finally got an easy call: transport an old man to the emergency hospital. We picked up the old man and his wife at their hotel and started the transport. On the wagon, you could hold onto the back with the aid of two bars by the door. If you paid attention, you could see trouble starting and hit the back of the wagon, causing the driver to slam on the brakes, thereby tumbling all inside to the front of the wagon. I was not paying attention and the old lady, for some unknown reason, pushed me off the back, where I was run over by a cab that was following us. My wife was brought to the hospital, as they did not know if I was going to make it. While they thought I was unconscious, I heard them discuss whether I was drunk or not. Thank God, I was not drinking that day, but I realized what my co-workers thought of me. I determined to change right then and there.

1 Peter 1:14
As obedient children, do not conform to the evil desires you had when you lived in ignorance.

Dan Says:
"We know what God wants from us. Do not wait for His adjustment in our lives."

# Moments of Ministry

# February 17

I have a wonderful friend named Owen. We try to get together several times a week. We enjoy playing pool together and always have time for good conversation after the game. At least twice a week, we enjoy studying the Word together and he has great insight that I often will use in my teaching. One day I asked Owen how to get to a certain address and the direction he gave me was as follows. "Go down Seltice Ave. and turn right where the red barn used to be." Now the information was true, but never having seen the red barn, it was useless. I am afraid that we, as Christians, do the same thing with unbelievers. We tell the truth, but with no background, it is of no use.

1 Timothy 3:9
They must keep hold of the deep truths of the faith with a clear conscience.

Dan Says:
"We must explain the truths of the faith in a clear, concise manner, so as not to cause confusion."

# Moments of Ministry

# February 18

To keep in shape and watch my weight, I walk. I have all the neighborhood distances measured, so I can know how far I walk. On one of my two-mile walks, I walk by a skate park. It is a concrete bowl with lots of contraptions that the skaters use to do tricks. One day, as I was walking by, I watched the youngsters do their fancy tricks. It was quite fascinating and very entertaining. I watched several do very fancy maneuvers and was amused, so I smiled and laughed at them. As I continued my walk, someone came up behind me and hit me on the shoulder. As I turned, I saw it was a skateboarder and a few of his friends. He said to me "you think it is funny that I fell"? He then proceeded to throw a punch at me. I saw it coming and moved my head so he would miss, but seeing as how I was a trained boxer, I threw my own punch that did not miss. As the young man lay on the ground, I asked if he wished to continue. He said, "No". Being a sixty-five year old pastor in the area, I hoped that no one saw the incident. No such luck. But good did come out of our misunderstanding, all the kids at the skate park now wave and say hello. Maybe God will use that connection some day.

1 Timothy 6:12
Fight the good fight of the faith. Take hold of the eternal life to which you were called when you made your good confession in the presence of many witnesses.

Dan Says:
"Your innocent actions can sometimes cause hurt to others. Not physical, but to hurt someone's pride can be very damaging."

# Moments
## of Ministry

## February 19

As I was driving home from the mission, where I was working, I kept noticing that many of the cars coming in the opposite direction were waving at me. I thought that everyone is sure friendly today and went my merry way. Now it became really noticeable as people were waving frantically at me. I checked all the gauges on my car and could see nothing wrong. I thought maybe my car was on fire, but I could see no smoke or flames, so on I continued. When I arrived home and parked in the driveway I saw the problem. Those fun loving boys at the mission had wired a life-sized doll under my bumper so as to appear I was dragging a child under the car. Who said that drunks and winos have no sense of humor? When I went to work at the gospel mission the next day I was the butt of many jokes. As I talked to Harry Altmeyer, the boss, he said, "Well they finally accepted you".

Romans 8:28
And we know that in all things God works for the good of those who love him, who have been called according to his purpose.

Dan Says:
"Love and acceptance can be shown in a variety of ways."

# MOMENTS OF MINISTRY

# February 20

Standing in the lineup for inspection, we were all surprised that the night supervising captain made an appearance. He said he wanted to ride with a dog unit and, as I was the only one, I was selected. No sooner had we hit the street, than we got a hot call. That means the there was a burglar trapped in a building and they wanted the dog to flush him out. When we arrived at the scene, I asked the Captain to wait outside as the dog gets very excited when he is working and has been known to attack even me. He replied that he would accompany me into the building; you don't argue with captains, so in we went. I used the commands for attack so the dog would search. He took off like a bullet. He went about thirty feet and turned and snarled and exposed his teeth and came back at us as fast as he could. I was now trying to get the situation in hand, but was having difficulty, as the captain was hanging around my neck. The dog went right on by us and attacked the burglar who was hiding behind the front door. We put him in custody and the captain told me to take him to the station. I said, "I have to get information for the arrest report", but he was insistent that we leave now. As we got into the car, I noticed that the captain had his hat covering his lap and then realized what the emergency was.

Proverbs 1:33
But whoever listens to me will live in safety and be at ease, without fear of harm.

Dan Says:
"We place ourselves in fearful situations when we do not listen to sound advice."

# Moments of Ministry

# February 21

I was not thrilled with my uniform at the Sheriff's Department; I thought it made me look like a priest. Though the uniform was brown and had the patches and all, it was the clerical collar that made me look that way. People would always call me "Father" and some even wanted to confess to me. When I told them that I would be happy to get an officer to whom they could confess, they would often get angry. One day, I went to visit a man at his workplace who was living with us. When I asked another employee to tell him I was there, he went to get him and said, "There is a 'preacher cop' wanting to talk to you." That title kind of stuck with me for a while. I guess it was all right, as that was what I was, sort of.

Galatians 2:6
As for those who were held in high esteem - whatever they were makes no difference to me; God does not show favoritism.

Dan Says:
"It is what you do, not what you look like."

# MOMENTS OF MINISTRY

# February 22

My mind and my heart were racing as fast as they could. I hung up the phone and tried to interpret the message I had just received. It was from a specialist to whom my doctor had referred me. He was a cancer specialist. The message was, "Could I make an appointment with him and bring my whole family?" My mind was spinning so fast I even forgot to pray. "What was the problem?" I thought, "Was I going to die soon?" All kinds of thoughts were going on in my head. With my family, we heard him say I had prostate cancer. He gave us all the options for treatment and we decided to just leave it in the Lord's hands. I am so glad that we did. I have had many years of healthy enjoyment in life.

Psalm 33:21
In him our hearts rejoice, for we trust in his holy name.

Dan Says:
"There is nothing on this earth that compares to trust in God."

# Moments
## of Ministry

# February 23

The outline began to appear in the dirt; whatever it was, the shape was round. I carefully began removing the soil around the object and soon it began to emerge. I had found an intact bowl; it was very small and fit in the palm of my hand. We took photos of the bowl before removing it from the dirt and took very precise measurements. Boy was I proud, the archeologist who was in charge of the dig came and inspected my find and announced that I had discovered an ancient votive offering bowl. A short time later in the morning, a visiting archeologist came by the area I was working, and seeing the bowl reached down and examined it. "I see you have found a salt shaker" he said. The man who wrote the report of the dig wanted to find significance in the bowl, while the other just found the mundane. It is all in the eye of the beholder and what he wants to see.

Matthew 5:17-48 (Summary)
Jesus often said "you have heard it said, but I tell you" He spoke to clear up a misunderstanding of the Old Testament that was interpreted wrongly by the Rabbis.

Dan Says:
"When you hear a new interpretation of the Word, be cautious and check carefully."

# MOMENTS OF MINISTRY

# February 24

There I was, standing if front of all the men at the mission, expounding on all that I had learned the day before at Bible School. I was so full of myself that I must have looked like a fool to the men. One day, as I was carefully explaining all of the Greek words to them and explaining in great detail all the verbiage I could muster about a simple passage, a man came up to me and said " I am going to quit reading the Bible". His statement shocked me, so I asked why he would do such a thing. He said he just read it and did not know that it was so hard to understand. Boy! Did I blow it! I asked for his forgiveness and said I was totally wrong in what I was doing and "would you forgive me?" He said he would and I never spoke over the head of anyone again at the mission.

1 Thessalonians 1:3
We remember before our God and Father your work produced by faith, your labor prompted by love, and your endurance inspired by hope in our Lord Jesus Christ.

Dan Says:
"When teaching God's Word, always remember to put the cookies on the bottom shelf!"

# Moments
## of Ministry

# February 25

We spotted the smoke in the old hotel and immediately ran inside. I took the top floor and my partner took the second floor. We ran door to door pounding on them and telling people to get out. One old lady said she could not leave her cat, when I picked it up; it was out of control scratching and clawing me. So I threw it out an open window and carried the old lady outside. While we were standing there, I noticed a man sitting on his window ledge on the third floor. I told him to stay put until I could get help. Instead he jumped; I ran over and attempted to catch him. We both hit the pavement. I was trying to get him to an ambulance when medical showed up on scene. They looked at him, and then placed me in the ambulance. I had crushed vertebrae in my back, torn my biceps muscle and tore the arm from my shoulder. I even hurt my leg. The jumper died at the scene.

Mark 14:47
Then one of those standing near drew his sword and struck the servant of the high priest, cutting off his ear.

Dan Says:
"It pays to think of the consequence before you take action."

# Moments of Ministry

# February 26

The phone rang and when I answered, it was an old friend who had moved out of the area. He wanted to play some golf, so I got us a starting time at a local course. We were playing along and talking about where he was attending church and how his life was going. We got to the third hole, a par three, and when it was my turn to drive the ball, I stepped up and hit a beauty. We watched as the ball arched high in the sky and finally landed in front of the green. The ball started to roll toward the hole and kept getting closer until it finally dropped into the hole. A hole in one! I was very proud and my friend was so excited he even called my pastor to tell him before we reached the hole. He asked, "Was that was the most exciting thing you have ever done?" I had to tell him it was not even close. I said, Try to lead someone to the Lord and then you can be really excited".

Acts 11:22-24
News of this reached the church in Jerusalem, and they sent Barnabas to Antioch. When he arrived and saw what the grace of God had done, he was glad and encouraged them all to remain true to the Lord with all their hearts. He was a good man, full of the Holy Spirit and faith, and a great number of people were brought to the Lord.

Dan Says:
"If you want to experience true joy, let the Lord use you to bring someone to Himself."

# MOMENTS
## OF MINISTRY

# February 27

The alarm went off and we responded to the sandwich shop again. We arrived and the man was there with a broom sweeping up the place. We asked him if he knew the alarm was going. He said "Oh that again. I will get it fixed". We proceeded on patrol and about a half an hour later we were asked once again to return to the sandwich shop. When we arrived there was a different man there. We asked him why we were back and he said we should search the shop. I explained that his employee was there when we came the first time. He said he had no employees at all. Boy that burglar was one cool cookie. We never did catch him.

Colossians 3:25
Anyone who does wrong will be repaid for their wrongs, and there is no favoritism.

Dan Says:
"You can fool man, but no way can you fool God."

# Moments of Ministry

# February 28

On the ship, it was decided that half of the ship's company could have off a few days for either Thanksgiving or Christmas. I went to the ship's officer in charge of leave and offered to stay for both, if I could have time off in February to take my girl to the prom. He said it was fine with him. When the time came for leave, I put in my request and was denied. So, I went home anyway. A deal is a deal. After I was home for a couple of weeks, some military police came to my house. I decided that it was time to return to the ship. They gave me a court martial, gave me a loss of pay and time in the brig. The worst of all was everyone was getting an early out of the service, but I could not get it because I had to make up brig time.

Jeremiah 17:10
"I the Lord search the heart and examine the mind, to reward each person according to their conduct, according to what their deeds deserve."

Dan Says:
"God is an understanding judge; I wish justice in the world were like His."

# MOMENTS OF MINISTRY

# February 29

Hearing the words "Cancer" and "Tumor" in the same sentence is very disturbing, especially if the doctor is talking about you. When I heard that statement, I was taken aback a little, as the same doctor had told me even thought I had cancer, I would probably die of something else. I was told to go to the Cancer Center and they would tell me what I had to do next. My wife and I knew what we had to next- pray about the whole situation. We went to the center and were advised of what treatment would be best for me. I have started the process and will continue to do as I am told, but I know that real healing will come from the Lord and I willing to accept whatever that is.

Isaiah 53:5
But he was pierced for our transgressions, he was crushed for our iniquities; the punishment that brought us peace was on him, and by his wounds we are healed.

Dan Says:
"All we really have is a trust that He will care for us."

# Moments
## of Ministry

# March 1

After working the midnight to eight in the morning watch, I used to go to the golf course and play nine holes. One day the starter asked if I would mind playing with an older lady, I said that was ok with me. As the game progressed I noticed that this woman kept hitting the ball right down the middle... She would then hit another shot short of the green, but close. Her pitching was excellent and man could she putt. Pretty soon I saw that she was giving me a good beating on the course. After we finished the round I went to the starter and asked whom I was playing with he said "Ken Venturi's mother". He was my favorite professional golfer and I know who his teacher was.

Proverbs 12:1
Whoever loves discipline loves knowledge, but he who hates correction is stupid

Dan Says:
"Listen to advice from Godly sources and you will prosper in all you do."

# Moments of Ministry

# March 2

One of my proudest moments as a police officer came in the form of an ordinary arrest. I was walking a beat in downtown San Francisco when I heard a scream as I ran toward the sound several people were pointing to a young man running. As I looked I could see he had a purse under his arm. The chase went on forever he was young and I was in full uniform, which meant that I had a gun belt and flashlight, handcuffs and radio on my waist and that slowed me down considerably. I just continued to run and keep him in sight after a long chase I finally caught him. They were building the Bart underground rail system and there was a large hole in the street. As I grabbed the young man he struggled and fell into the hole. This was at commute time so the street was very crowded. I thought that I would surely receive some complaints. Instead the whole crowd gave me an ovation.

Ephesians 2:3
All of us also lived among them at one time, gratifying the cravings of our flesh and following its desires and thoughts. Like the rest, we were by nature deserving of wrath.

Dan Says:
"Sometimes we are an object of wrath, not only in God's eyes, but in others as well."

# MOMENTS
## OF MINISTRY

# March 3

We were sitting at the prosecutors' table listening to the older lady testify about the arrest that I had made during a riot. She said that I had beaten her son with my riot stick and also his little daughter. She was in tears and the jury was looking like they wanted to convict me instead of the defendant. I poked the district attorney and said say something before I get hung out to dry. He said not to worry as he had it under control. I did not think so and was sweating thinking that I would soon be indicted for gross misconduct. When the time for cross-examination came the attorney said he would just ask one question. Fine I thought now its jail for me for sure. He looked at the woman and asked, "Are you related to the defense attorney?" She said she was his mother. The judge then stopped the proceedings and had her and her son arrested on the spot. Boy was I relieved and thankful.

John 8:44
You belong to your father, the devil, and you want to carry out your father's desires. He was a murderer from the beginning, not holding to the truth, for there is no truth in him. When he lies, he speaks his native language, for he is a liar and the father of lies.

Dan Says:
"Do what is right and tell the truth and in the end the truth will win out."

# MOMENTS
## OF MINISTRY

# March 4

Going into ministry at an older age was very difficult. When you have grey hair people expect you to know more. As a matter of fact I did know more than the younger students at the Bible College. But most of my experience would be rated very secular. Most of my experiences were things not to do. I was very fortunate to have some wonderful mentors. These men who were even older than I was had lots of ministry experience. All my advisors, the ones who were most useful, were my family, my daughters, and especially my wife. These people loved me and wanted the best for me all the time. And I could trust their judgments.

Proverbs 4:5
Get wisdom, get understanding; do not forget my words or turn away from them.

Dan Says:
"If you have Godly people in your family, get wisdom from them first, because they care about you."

# Moments of Ministry

# March 5

My wife, the two boys living with us, and I all marched into the small church where I was guest speaking and took seats right down in front. I thought it was strange that we were not greeted or someone did not come to introduce themselves. My wife opened her bulletin and then said to me "honey I think we are in the wrong church". I looked and sure enough there was no mention of a guest speaker. Whoops we got up and sheepishly walked out and found the right church up the street. The man who introduced us said Thank God I did not think we could sing another song. The two young men who lived with us had many days of pleasure telling all who would listen about my blunder.

Proverbs 17:22
A cheerful heart is good medicine, but a crushed spirit dries up the bones.

Dan Says:
"When you accidentally do something wrong try getting some joy from it."

# Moments
## of Ministry

# March 6

Moving from the San Francisco bay area to northern Idaho was a BIG culture shock. There were no sidewalks in front of my house, people smiled at you for no reason even if you did not know them. The biggest change of all was how a man was judged in this part of the country was the size of his woodpile. I soon learned all the tricks to get free wood, go to the mill dump and get all the log ends and use them. But we often went into the woods to gather wood. It is a miracle that I was able to come back alive. More than once a tree tried to do me in, but I was too fast. I also nearly dropped a big tree on my truck once. I guess because the Lord loved me He allowed me to survive. It was sure nice to have gas come up our street so we no longer had to use a wood fire. But it is not nearly so exciting now.

Habakkuk 2:13
Has not the Lord Almighty determined that the people's labor is only fuel for the fire, that the nations exhaust themselves for nothing?

Dan Says:
"When the work is done and the fire done all that remains is ash. But you do have the heat and the memories of the gathering and the good time in the warmth of the stove."

# MOMENTS OF MINISTRY

# March 7

My grandson was coming on his first fishing adventure with the men. We were going up on the river and there was no place to eat so we stopped at my favorite café to load up on some vittles. After a good day on the river catching fish and having great fun, we headed back to town. I could hardly wait for the report that Josh was going to give his Mom and Dad about the trip. This is what he said, "we stopped to eat and the waitress came with both arms filled with plates of food. And that was just for Grandpa!" You never know what to expect from a child when you give him a new experience.

Proverbs 15:17
Better a small serving of vegetables with love than a fattened calf with hatred.

Dan Says:
"When we take our children and attempt to teach them something, the lesson they learn is how we live our lives not what we say."

# MOMENTS
## OF MINISTRY

# March 8

Not again! This was the sixth time I had arrested him and brought him to court. Just to hear the Judge let him go again. This criminal was a "wolf", that is a man who ripped off pensioners of their social security checks. I stood up in court and said, "You have sentenced this man to death". The judge asked what I meant and I said next time I catch this guy I am going to throw him off a pier and not bring him to court. The judge held me in contempt and had me arrested. As I was sitting drinking coffee with the jailers we were told the judge wanted to see me in his chambers. He said he would take an apology and let me go. I said I would rather take the case to the newspapers. He let me go and said for me not to discuss this, case with anyone.

Acts 4:20
"As for us, we cannot help speaking about what we have seen and heard."

Dan Says:
"Authority should be from God, but we do have a Christian responsibility to seek the truth."

# Moments
## of Ministry

# March 9

Here I was alone with two little kids their Mother said she and Grandma would only be gone a couple of hours. She might as well as said months. What was I to do? Then Amy said, "let's have a tea party". I brightened right up and ran to the car to get the supplies for our tee party. From the car I got a couple of putters and some golf balls. We set up a course in the house, down the stairs, round the corner, under tables all over the house. We laughed and had wonderful time then the door opened and there was Dannell and G'Ma. The time flew by and the mess was minimal.

Psalm 68:3
But may the righteous be glad and rejoice before God: may they be happy and joyful.

Dan Says:
"True joy comes when you enjoy the family that God has gifted you with."

# Moments
## of Ministry

# March 10

Being the youngest boy was hard, but for me even worse as I was born on the same day as my older brother. He always had older kids around at the party spoiling it for us young ones. But life has a way of evening up things. When he was a teen he had a party with a bunch of young kids around who loved to spy on the older ones and tell mom everything they were doing. As we got older we reached the point where we enjoyed our birthdays together. We learned to share and get along eventually we even began to get the same presents from everyone. But the one thing that always was special for me on my birthday was PASTIES the most delicious meat pie you ever tasted.

Acts 4:32
All the believers were one in heart and mind. No one claimed that any of their possessions was their own, but they shared everything they had.

Dan Says:
"The best part of sharing is the feeling of love that it evokes."

# Moments of Ministry

# March 11

I do not know of anyone who is as fortunate as I am in baptizing their family. I have had the privilege of baptizing my children and my grandchildren in the Jordan River. I have had the opportunity to travel to Israel Many times and baptize many people where Jesus was baptized. It never fails to amaze me how people respond to the experience some weep some are so excited that I think they can walk on the water. But they all seem to be different when they come out. Now I do not think that there is some magic or wonderful miracle that happens. But I do believe that God does change people through the sacrament of baptism. He seems to place in their hearts the knowledge that they are now different. They have taken the step of obedience to his command. And they can feel His joy. When my wife came up out of the water she radiated with the love and joy of Christ.

Matthew 3:16-17
As soon as Jesus was baptized, he went up out of the water. At that moment heaven was opened, and he saw the Spirit of God descending like a dove and alighting on him. 17 And a voice from heaven said, "This is my Son, whom I love; with him I am well pleased."

Dan Says:
"God gets great joy in our obedience."

# Moments
## of Ministry

# March 12

Being a good Grandpa is harder than it looks. I did enjoy going to all of my grandson's games. The hockey was cold, but you could usually get a cup of coffee to keep warm. The other sports baseball, soccer, and track were warmer sports and so more enjoyable. I could not just be supportive to Josh and not Amy. Amy was more artistic than sporty so she took dance lessons. I used to go pick her up and enjoyed watching her learn to dance. But there was this event called recitals in which a lot of girls would dance. It seemed like there were hundreds of them, not really, but it felt like it. They would go on and on until I thought I would die. In fact once I told her I would give her a hundred dollars if I could miss her performance. She said no deal. I hope now she realizes how much I loved her to sit through that torture.

1 John 3:18
Dear children, let us not love with words or speech but with actions and in truth.

Dan Says:
"You can say it all you want but kids want to see it in action."

# MOMENTS OF MINISTRY

# March 13

We got the call of the alarm going off at Sees Candy Factory. When we arrived I got the dog out of the wagon and was getting him ready for the search, but he was already so excited that I could hardly believe it. He was straining at the quick release leash and pulling me along. I knew he had a great smell going so as I entered the store I let him go and he immediately ran to a bin of chocolates and began to eat. I had a hard time pulling him away and he was growling at me the whole time. The storeowner had been looking through the window and I was sure he would be angry. Instead he said he wished he had a movie it would sell lots of candy. I guess it depends on who is looking how they decide if something is right or wrong. This time the temptation was too great to resist.

1 Corinthians 10:13
No temptation has overtaken you except what is common to mankind. And God is faithful; he will not let you be tempted beyond what you can bear. But when you are tempted, he will also provide a way out so that you can endure it.

Dan Says:
"If you put yourself where Satan can get you he probably will."

# Moments
## of Ministry

# March 14

Growing up in San Francisco in the forties and fifties was really great. We had very ethnic neighborhoods and they were well defined by street. Sometimes one side was Mexican and the other was Irish. We guarded our borders more than some nations. If you got caught in the other neighborhood you stood the chance of a beating or worse. But there were times when it was all right to trespass, maybe you had to play a baseball game or even go to a different church function. I remember one time running home being chased by a gang. I was fortunate my brother and some of his friends came to my rescue. It is so important to have a safe place to run to, even when we are old and grey. That place is still home and church. My family is always dependable and both are places where love is found.

2 Corinthians 13:11
Finally, brothers and sisters, rejoice! Strive for full restoration, encourage one another, be of one mind, live in peace. And the God of love and peace will be with you.

Dan Says:
"When trouble comes your way, run; do not walk, to the place where you can find peace and love. Run to your family and your church."

# Moments of Ministry

# March 15

Life in the navy was going very well for me; I had an easy job and was enjoying being a fighter for the Thirteenth Naval District. Then Willie Mays came into the service and messed it up for all the athletes. They had the Mays rule: you could not be in just one sport. One of the coaches came up with a brilliant idea and selected me to be a basketball player. Now that was very strange as I was five foot nine and only weighed one hundred and thirty eight pounds. But when he explained it made perfect sense my job was to get the best player on the other team into a fight and we would both get thrown out of the game. It worked for a while but pretty soon the other teams got wise. I then began to get really knocked around and the game was no longer fun.

Proverbs 14:12
There is a way that appears to be right, but in the end it leads to death.

Dan Says:
"When you keep bending the rules sometimes it is you that gets broke."

# MOMENTS
## OF MINISTRY

# March 16

We were in the yard working when our very old dog Millie decided to come out on the porch and sit in the sun. While we were busy we suddenly heard a thump and when we looked over we saw Millie on the rock patio, she had rolled over and had fallen off the porch. It was about a six foot drop and she was not responding to our desperate attempts to revive her. I sadly went into the garden shed to get a shovel to bury her. As I approached her she lifted her head, looked at the shovel gave me a dirty look and went back upstairs. We laughed and many jokes were made about not having me check the body should anyone die.

John 11:43
When he had said this, Jesus called in a loud voice, "Lazarus, come out!"

Dan Says:
"The Lord is the one who decides when death will come, but while you are here do His work."

# Moments
## of Ministry

# March 17

We had people over for dinner and were sitting at the table after we had eaten we were talking and having a good time. Our daughter came out of the bathroom and said that the toilet was acting up again. I immediately went and got my hammer to fix it. Sam who was our guest said to Maxine "what is he doing with the hammer?" Her reply was "he fixes everything with a hammer". No need to tell you I busted the tank on the toilet and it had to be replaced by a plumber. You see I always thought if it does not work beat it. Not the recipe for a good handyman, but it fit my personality perfectly. That method did not work with people when I became a pastor, but sometimes in my heart I just wanted to hit them with a hammer to fix them.

Proverbs 16:16
How much better to get wisdom than gold, to get insight rather than silver!

Dan Says:
"When you are a pastor and you want to fix people the hammer never works, but The Word of God always does."

# Moments
## of Ministry

# March 18

Before we opened the new jail, the Sheriff decided that it would be good to have a shakedown to see if everything worked. I invited some friends to spend the night and even get a t-shirt that read, "I was booked at Spokane County Jail". The men and women were separated and it was interesting to see what happened. The women went from cell to cell praying for the inmate who would be housed there. The men meantime tricked the guard by saying the shower was broken, when he went to check we jammed the door shut trapping him inside and then we ordered pizza from his phone. When we went to breakfast the next morning we were properly chastised for our behavior.

Isaiah 28:6
He will be a spirit of justice to the one who sits in judgment, a source of strength to those who turn back the battle at the gate.

Dan Says:
"Those women turned back evil at the door. God will be proud of their efforts. I wonder what He thought about us men."

# Moments of Ministry

# March 19

As we were growing up I began to look more and more like my older brother. People often mistook one for the other if we were not together. I would even make dates for my brother and not tell him. I was telling my brother about a restaurant that was really good. I had caught a robber coming out of the restaurant one day with the owner's wife as his hostage. I arrested the robber and set the wife free. When I would go back to eat at this place, no matter what I ordered I got a rib eye steak with it. My brother took his family to the restaurant and when the waitress came he ordered coffee and she said, "You know where the pot is get your own coffee". Then when his order of ravioli came it had a steak with it, he complained and the owner Fat Ed came out to see what was wrong. When they straightened out everything Jack had a free dinner and they all had a good laugh.

3 John 1:11
Dear friend, do not imitate what is evil but what is good. Anyone who does what is good is from God. Anyone who does what is evil has not seen God.

Dan Says:
"Do not pretend to be a Christian, just be one."

# MOMENTS OF MINISTRY

# March 20

There she stood, a vision of loveliness, she was wearing a grey poodle skirt and a white blouse and a red sweater. I was dressed in my best sport coat with a red tie and shined shoes. This was to be her first date; I had brought flowers and everything. Her mother took our photo and it seemed she was happy also. We went to the best restaurant in town and she got to order what ever she wanted. Everyone who saw her commented on how wonderful she looked. When we got home she proudly announced that her Grandpa had taken her on the best date ever. I certainly felt the same way I was never prouder to have a beautiful girl on my arm. I pray that little Amy will have a memory of how precious she was as a five year old with a grateful Grandpa.

Proverbs 25:11
Like apples of gold in settings of silver is a ruling rightly given.

Dan Says:
"Good memories are worth much more than wealth to leave your family."

# Moments of Ministry

# March 21

My daughter's boy friend said that he could get me a truckload of birch wood. Everyone knows it's the best wood for a wood stove. So we loaded up all of our wood cutting equipment and started off for the woods. We went up a dirt road and around a gate and I asked if we had permission. Rich answered, "Sure no problem I know the owner. Soon we were dropping trees all over the place. I felt a tap on my shoulder and as I turned there stood a stranger. He asked what was I doing and I said gathering firewood. He asked if I had permission and I said sure I was here with Rich. When he asked whom Rich was I knew I was in trouble. I told him the story and he said to buck up the wood I had down and get off his property. I was not very happy with Rich and was glad that the man did not prosecute us.

Jeremiah 9:5
Friend deceives friend, and no one speaks the truth. They have taught their tongues to lie; they weary themselves with sinning.

Dan Says:
"Trust is something that is earned and should not be given without thought and prayer."

# Moments of Ministry

## March 22

We all were getting in line to make the trip to the coast. There were police cars from every jurisdiction and the state police were also there. We all were going to a funeral of four police officers that were killed in Western Washington. I have never seen so many police in one place there were thousands of them. It was a very moving ceremony and we were all touched. I saw in the stadium a contingent of officers from San Francisco. I went over to talk with them and told them I was retired from the San Francisco Police Department. They asked when I retired and when I said sixty-seven they replied that none of them were born yet. Boy, talk about feeling old. As I related the story to our men on the way home, they reminded me I was older than dirt.

Philippians 1:3
I thank my God every time I remember you.

Dan Says:
"Your legacy is really just the good you leave behind."

# MOMENTS
## OF MINISTRY

# March 23

We went to a small out of the way campground named Indian Grinding Rock State Park. While lunch was being prepared my youngest daughter and I went for a walk. Colleen was about ten years old at that time. We spotted a sign way out in a field and decided to go and see what it said. We finally came close enough to read the sign, my daughter read it first and came running to me and jumped into my arms crying. There was no way her feet would touch the ground again. You see the sign read "Watch Out for Rattle Snakes". I am very fearful of snakes myself so it was a very fast trip back to the car where we ate lunch inside the vehicle.

Acts 28:5
But Paul shook the snake off into the fire and suffered no ill effects.

Dan Says:
"Stay away from snakes. The last time anyone listened to one we all got in trouble."

# Moments
## of Ministry

# March 24

We moved to Idaho and were no longer city folk. We were now self sufficient and very much outdoor types. It would almost be a sin to spend money on a Christmas tree when the hills around us were full of trees. This year we were going to get a free tree. Then trouble began first we had to get a six dollars permit. Then the battery on the truck failed so fifty dollars for a new one. Now we are all hungry off to Wendy's for lunch so fifteen more dollars. After finding the perfect tree, we came back to the truck and the parking brake had frozen, you guessed it fifty bucks for a tow truck. Our total that day was one hundred and twenty one dollars for a free tree. Next year twenty bucks off the lot sounds good to me.

Nahum 1:7
"The Lord is good, a refuge in times of trouble. He cares for those who trust in him,"

Dan Says:
"If your only desire is to save money, it could cost you all you have."

# Moments of Ministry

# March 25

Here I was lying in the doorway with a paper bag and a wine bottle sticking out of it and a ten-dollar bill falling out of my pocket. I kept wishing someone would come by and rob me soon as the doorway was cold. I had already arrested three others that night and one more would be enough. Sure enough here came a guy and looking around and seeing no one he reached down to remove the money. I came to my feet and told him he was under arrest and he decided to fight. We were going at it pretty good when suddenly I was looking up from the sidewalk. There standing over me was a good friend and fellow police officer who said he did not recognize me with his club in his hand. The bad guy went to jail and I went to the emergency room where they found no damage. I had known this officer all the way back in high school but he swore he did not know it was me.

Psalm 143:9
Rescue me from my enemies, Lord, for I hide myself in you.

Dan Says:
"If you look for enemies you find enemies but if you look for friends you find joy."

# Moments
## of Ministry

# March 26

I have a temper that is as bad as you can get. One time I was working on a car and after many weeks of taking apart and putting back together I was sure that it was right. I had changed the transmission from automatic to a four on the floor. It was mercury and was going to be the best car ever. We lived on a steep hill in San Francisco, so I thought that if I started down the hill and popped the clutch it would start right up. Down the hill I went and let go of the clutch and the whole transmission fell from the car. I went home and got a sledgehammer and was in the process of beating the car to death, when the police showed up. I said it was my car and I could beat it if I wanted. They shrugged and said, "Be sure to clean up".

Psalm 30:5
For his anger lasts only a moment, but his favor lasts a lifetime; weeping may stay for the night, but rejoicing comes in the morning.

Dan Says:
"A lost temper only causes pain and suffering and loss of esteem."

# Moments of Ministry

# March 27

I was a little tyke just old enough to let outside as long as I stayed on the block. My mother said there was nothing I could get into as we lived in a poor neighborhood in a mining town. But I was able to get everyone in our block mad as could be I had gone from house to house after the milk man and had drank the cream out of every bottle. The milk in those days was in a bottle with a bubble on top where the cream was; you could use it or shake the bottle and have a very rich milk. You could also make butter out of the cream. Well, needless to say I got a good spanking for my escapade and some people got the first taste of two percent milk.

Micah 6:14
You will eat but not be satisfied; your stomach will still be empty. You will store up but save nothing, because what you save I will give to the sword.

Dan Says:
"When you take away the best and leave the rest you are a pest."

# Moments
## of Ministry

# March 28

There it did it again. I just wanted to take a baseball bat and smack the computer. I decided to take a walk around the parking lot to cool down. Back at that dreaded machine again, I tried once more. The machine went and did it again. I rushed to the office of the computer guru Chris and told him to fix that bloody machine RIGHT NOW!!!!!! He calmly asked me what I was trying to do and I said I wanted to work in the book of Romans. He said try again and I had the same result. He said, "I know what the problem is, do you always spell Romans with a "P"? When he stopped laughing, he wandered off to tell anyone who would listen of my stupid error.

Proverbs 14:18
The simple inherit folly, but the prudent are crowned with knowledge.

Dan Says:
"Even your mistakes can bring much joy to others."

# Moments of Ministry

# March 29

My team was often used to make an entry when there was a raid of a dope dealer. On one occasion we were to secure the premises on a big dealer in the Haight-Ashbury District. A television crew got wind of the raid and was there when we arrived. We told them that once every thing was secure they could enter and film. I had split my team and my guys were coming into the back door. While we were waiting for the scheduled time to make entry nature called and I had to go to the bathroom right now. So my team went in early, I ran right to the bathroom and was doing business when there was a great pounding on the door, I called out that I was in there, but they broke down the door and there I was and the television crew was filming. I was so embarrassed. I bet you can guess what video was played at my retirement.

Proverbs 29:23
Pride brings a person low, but the lowly in spirit gain honor.

Dan Says:
"The best laid plans often go astray, but if you do things God's way you will win in the end."

# Moments of Ministry

# March 30

My friend had a gentleman farm in the country and had decided to put in a fishpond. I helped him all I could and soon we had a great little pond. Well he had it stocked with Capitals West Bank Cut Throat Trout. They grew to be good-sized fish and he used it to entertain guests. The fish were fed Purina Fish Chow and would come to the edge of the pond if anyone approached. Well my brother had come to visit from California and I had made arrangements with my friend to fish the pond for some fish to eat. As we came down the road I told my brother that sometimes farmers would let us fish in their ponds. When we started fishing he caught fish on every cast. He was astounded at how good the fishing was. I said it is like this all over Idaho. He went home believing that was true.

Ephesians 5:6
Let no one deceive you with empty words, for because of such things God's wrath comes on those who are disobedient.

Dan Says:
"A deceiver can be anyone, even a trusted friend or relative."

# Moments of Ministry

# March 31

Shooting field archery was a very special sport. You walked through some woods and shoot arrows at various sized targets and all at different distances. Well archery became a sport in the Police Olympics and I decided to enter. I won the gold medal and took a lot of good nature kidding in the department. Usually the Bow and Arrow Squad was a term for someone who had their gun taken away and given a desk job. One of the guys on the bomb squad thought he had a wonderful idea; we would load an aluminum arrow with explosives and fix the point so when it hit something it would explode. We got a call to the projects in the Fillmore District to apprehend a suspect who was shooting at a firehouse. The door to the bad guy's apartment was at the end of a hallway. I was talked into using the arrow on the door, I shot and all of a sudden the arrow hit the door turned around and came back at the squad. We all hit the floor and the explosive arrow simply turned to dust. We realized that the door was made of metal too late.

James 3:13
Who is wise and understanding among you? Let them show it by their good life, by deeds done in the humility that comes from wisdom.

Dan Says:
"The difference between knowledge and wisdom is, knowledge is the gathering of facts. Wisdom is knowing how to use the facts for Gods glory."

# Moments of Ministry

# April 1

As we travelled down the road to the edge of the wilderness I saw what was obviously a prison. We stopped the car and I got out to take some photos because I was a Chaplain in a jail and was interested in their system of incarceration. We were driving down the road minding our own business when suddenly the car began to shake and move all over the road. I had no idea of what was happening and then a jet airplane not fifty feet off the ground passed over us. I got control of the car and pulled to the side of the road. Soon a police car pulled us over and I was wondering what I had done. They explained that in Israel you do not take photos of the maximum security prison. I thanked them and asked if they wanted my film. They said, "No, but please be more cautious in the future".

I Thessalonians 4:11
and to make it your ambition to lead a quiet life: You should mind your own business and work with your hands, just as we told you,

Dan Says:
"Sometimes when we think we are minding our own business we really are not."

# MOMENTS
## OF MINISTRY

# April 2

Mack sure looked the part; we had gone out the day before and bought him all he needed to fly fish. Now we were walking along the banks of the Little North Fork River, I brought him here because there were lots of little fish and I wanted him to have a good experience. As I explained how to read the river and not fish where there were not any fish to be had he suddenly had his line straightened out and the fight began. I could not believe my eyes the fish flashed a couple of times and I could see it was huge. Well he finally landed the fish and as we let it go I thought that was really too bad. You see he will spend the next twenty years trying to duplicate that catch. He did not know and when he said that was easy, I could only nod and laugh to myself. You see he will spend the next twenty years trying to duplicate that catch.

Luke 5:9
For he and all his companions were astonished at the catch of fish they had taken

Dan Says:
"To master anything, take time to learn how to do it correctly."

# Moments
## of Ministry

# April 3

At the garage sale I spotted it, a perfect teaching pot. Now you might ask what a teaching pot is. Sometimes I got the chance to teach archeology in the schools. One of my favorite things to do is to show my artifact collection. I show slides of how a dig is conducted in a very scientific way so we can put it back together on paper. When I was teaching at a grammar school one of my favorite things to bring is a pot of clay and when I hand it to a student I deliberately drop it. I do this so I can have them put the pot back together like an archeologist does. As I handed the pot to a little girl I let it drop to the floor and shatter. I was not prepared for what happened next. She began to weep and I had a hard time consoling her and explaining what I had done. The teacher had the children gather the pieces of pot and they said they would fix it. After some time I was asked to return and when I did the teacher and the little girl presented me with the pot that they had glued back together. They had placed some candy inside the pot in such a way that the only way to get it was to break the pot. I held it high and let it fall and said, "Let's eat".

2 Timothy 2:20
In a large house there are articles not only of gold and silver, but also of wood and clay; some are for special purposes and some for common use.

Dan Says:
"Do not blame the pot for its misuse, and do not blame the Word when it is misused to deceive."

# Moments of Ministry

# April 4

My family and I were on a jungle adventure day in Kauai we would kayak up a river and then trek in the jungle. We would swing on a rope and jump into a waterfall and even go down a zip line over a river. Then we would tour where many movies were made. It sounded like fun so we arrived at the river and were assigned our kayaks my wife, granddaughter Amy and I were in together and as we started up the river it became apparent that we did not know what we were doing. The guide came alongside and tried to instruct us, but we just got worse. We were doing military boating right, left, right, and left. It was decided to change people in the boat my wife got out and was replaced by my daughter. My wife took off up river with her new partner and I still was all over the river. It was not her, it was me. I finally saw a motorboat and asked if we could hold on and get to our destination. It was very embarrassing, but we did get to ride in a motorboat back down river.

1 Corinthians 7:34
…But a married woman is concerned about the affairs of this world—how she can please her husband.

Dan Says:
"Even if life takes some strange turns stick it out and enjoy the ride."

# Moments of Ministry

# April 5

When a 406 call comes on the police radio it means that there is a police officer in so much trouble that he needs help right now. We were on the Embaracado when the call came in. It was on the docks and about three miles away I really got into the gas pedal and we were doing over ninety miles an hour when we hit top speed. We got to the right pier and saw several stevedores surrounding two officers who were attempting to make an arrest. When we rolled up I jumped out and ran to the officer I noticed that my partner did not exit the car and wondered why. Soon other cars came and we had a superior force and were able to extract the officers and their prisoner. Getting back into the car my partner said to take him back to the station. When we arrived he told the watch commander that he would never get into a car with me again. I was surprised and asked him why and he said I went too fast to the call. I asked him how fast I should come when he called for help.

1 Corinthians 7:17
Nevertheless, each person should live as a believer in whatever situation the Lord has assigned to them, just as God has called them.

Dan Says:
"If you can't go all the way, don't go at all."

# Moments of Ministry

# April 6

Walking up from the water on beautiful Poipu beach I noticed that my wife and daughters were looking very strangely at me. As I came closer my wife said to put a towel around my waist. I asked what could possibly be the matter and again my wife said to cover myself up. I looked down at my swim shorts and saw what the problem was. The swim shorts that I bought at a bargain were camouflage. But that wasn't the problem. What I failed to realize is that when the material of my new swim shorts got wet, images of naked women appeared on my shorts. What made it worse was that I was wearing a tee shirt that read, "Church is a Team Sport" from my home church. I am sure that people who saw me were getting a confusing message.

1 Corinthians 4:4
My conscience is clear, but that does not make me innocent. It is the Lord who judges me.

Dan Says:
"When you advertise your faith, make sure your walk is in order."

# MOMENTS OF MINISTRY

# April 7

I was walking my beat in Japan Town a part of San Francisco that is mostly Japanese restaurants and hotels. This is a very easy beat as the culture of the area is very lawful and hardly ever reports any crime. If there is a crime the people take care of the problem themselves. So I was surprised when a hotel manager asked to see me to make a police report. It seems that some businessmen from Japan were in town conducting a large buy of equipment. They had had some drinks in the bar and invited two ladies to come up to their room. The women asked the men to shower and when they did the women stole a briefcase, and their wallets. When asked what the briefcase contained they replied thirty thousand dollars in cash. I went down to the nearest bar and as I was approaching the girls waved to me to stop. They thought that they had stolen dope money and wanted to give it back. So all was restored and the men were very grateful, and I became a hero on the beat.

Romans 13:12
The night is nearly over; the day is almost here. So let us put aside the deeds of darkness and put on the armor of light.

Dan Says:
"Love in the wrong place could be very costly so only love what is good."

# Moments of Ministry

# April 8

Here we were on the streets of Rome I could hardly believe it. We had just come out of the Vatican and had seen endless treasures. The one thing that impressed me more than anything else in the Vatican was the number of pickpockets. I used to work the pickpocket detail in San Francisco during the Christmas rush, so I was aware of them. Well Maxine and I came around a corner and there was a Pizza Truck, I got very excited and could not wait to have a pizza in Rome. When I ordered the man took a slice of bread and put some sauce on it and warmed it in an oven and gave it to me. It was terrible; I have never been so disappointed in anything. We did however have a wonderful dinner at our hotel.

Proverbs 10:3
The Lord does not let the righteous go hungry, but he thwarts the craving of the wicked.

Dan Says:
"God will provide, but it is not always sirloin steak."

# Moments
## of Ministry

# April 9

We were driving a plain car in the Haight district when my partner spotted a girl get out of a Volkswagen bus with an armload of rifles. We watched which house she entered and called for the rest of the team. We knocked on the door and when she answered she called out to others in the house "it's the pigs". Several individuals attempted to exit by the rear door, but were easily captured by our team outside. The thing that was really scary about this arrest was not the abundance of weapons, but the literature that we found. It described how to demoralize a society by the killing of police and other public officials. According to what was written you can best bring down a society by the slaughter of their children. What a bunch of crazy maniacs we lucked into before they could carry out their plans.

Matthew 19:14
Jesus said, "Let the little children come to me, and do not hinder them, for the kingdom of heaven belongs to such as these."

Dan Says:
"What Jesus loves, Satan hates. Do not allow him to get our most precious resource."

# Moments of Ministry

# April 10

It was a glorious day; we were playing on a fancy golf course. My brother had somehow gotten us an invitation to play and we were thrilled. We even got to ride for the first time in a golf cart. It was a three-wheeled affair with one wheel in the front. We each took turns driving and what fun it was. Here we were with the "hoity-toity" wealthy people that we had caddied for in the past. We were riding high on the hog. When we were approaching the last hole, I was one stroke up on Jack. He hit his ball to the green and all I had to do was match his shot. Then disaster struck. I hit my shot into some water and was I ever angry. I swung my club and hit the front tire of the cart. The club hit the rubber and came back twice the speed and hit me on the toe breaking it. I doubled over in pain and Jack doubled over in laughter. If I could have chased him he was next to get hit with the club. From utter joy to disaster in a moment of time.

Matthew 8:26
He replied, "You of little faith, why are you so afraid?" Then he got up and rebuked the winds and the waves, and it was completely calm.

Dan Says:
"Everything can change in one minute when God intervenes."


# MOMENTS
## OF MINISTRY

# April 11

When my father passed away and the funeral director contacted the Veterans Administration we were all surprised that they wanted to bury my dad at Arlington National cemetery. My mom said no because she wanted him closer so she could visit the gravesite. We were also surprised to get a letter from the President when he passed. I asked one of my friends who was a military buff if he could see why all the fuss. He checked and related to me what happened. My father was in the navy on a military transport that was bringing troops to France during World War One. The Montana Regiment showed up on his ship to be transported and when they got off my father got off with them. He received the Legion of Honor from the French Government and a Silver Star from the United States Army. When he was discharged they decided that he was not a deserter but a hero. So he received and honorable discharge from both the Army and the Navy.

1 Corinthians 10:33
…For I am not seeking my own good but the good of many, so that they may be saved.

Dan Says:
"Love is the ability to give it all you got all the time."

# Moments
## of Ministry

# April 12

While riding on camels to the great pyramid in Egypt I was surprised to hear "Dan, Dan"! I was wondering whom I could possibly know here in Ginza. As I got off the camel, there was an Arab asking me for money. He knew my name and I was wondering how he was aware of who I was. It seems that he talked my wife into letting him take her photo on the camel, but now wanted five dollars to give back the camera. Amy said I had all the money so he came to me. I informed him that if he did not want to visit the local hospital he should give me my camera. He complied and then I felt sorry for the gruff manner I had used with him so I gave him a dollar. Everyone we met in Egypt seemed intent on getting money from us in any way possible.

Luke 12:15
Then he said to them, "Watch out! Be on your guard against all kinds of greed; life does not consist in an abundance of possessions."

Dan Says:
"Wealth is a worry to some and a blessing to others who share."

# Moments of Ministry

# April 13

Here I was lying in the doorway with a paper bag and a wine bottle sticking out of it and a ten dollar bill falling out of my pocket. I wished someone would come by and rob me soon as the doorway was cold. I had already arrested three others that night and one more would be enough. Sure enough, here came a guy walking by. He was looking everywhere and after seeing no one around he reached down to remove the money. I came to my feet and told him he was under arrest and he decided to fight. We were going at it pretty good when suddenly I was looking up from the sidewalk. There standing over me, with a club in his hand, was a good friend and fellow police officer who said he did not recognize me. The bad guy went to jail and I went to the emergency room where they found no damage. I had known this office all the way back in high school but he swore he not know it was me.

Psalm 143:9
Rescue me from my enemies, Lord, for I hide myself in you.

Dan Says:
"If you look for enemies, you find enemies. If you look for friends, you find joy."

# Moments of Ministry

# April 14

Working in the Haight-Ashbury neighborhood undercover was always interesting. I had offers to join every religion on the planet and some were way out there. I would sometimes talk to the person to pass the time. On one occasion I was discussing this person's faith when he said they had the best "grass" in the world and I could get all I wanted. This was interesting to me and I asked where they kept this huge stash. He said, "The safest place in the world". I asked where that would be and he told me, "the church basement". He informed me that police were not allowed to search places of worship so it was absolutely safe. I got the address and when we showed up with a search warrant the man asked, "Can't you read?". There was a hand painted sign that said "CHURCH". The court did not recognize that sign as signifying the facility as a place of worship. One thing I can say is that they were "happy worshipers".

Hebrews 10:24-25
And let us consider how we may spur one another on toward love and good deeds, not giving up meeting together, as some are in the habit of doing, but encouraging one another

Dan Says:
"The safest place on earth is the church of Jesus Christ."

# MOMENTS
## OF MINISTRY

# April 15

The young kindergarten teacher was relating a story to us and we laughed until tears came. It seems that she was reading a picture book to the children that was filled with all kinds of animals. As she turned each page she would ask the children to identify each animal. She turned one page and asked what this animal is and a young boy answered her "it is a fricken elephant". She was shocked and said that we do not speak like that in Christian schools. He was very insistent he was right so she finally said to bring in the book. He came in the next day and showed her the book and the page said African Elephant he said "see a fricken elephant". I guess it is all in the pronunciation.

2 Timothy 2:15
Do your best to present yourself to God as one approved, a worker who does not need to be ashamed and who correctly handles the word of truth.

Dan Says:
"Sometimes what you think is true is not at all."

# Moments
## of Ministry

# April 16

We were at the archeological site at Arad; I had grabbed my food and made it into a sandwich. I just wanted some time to be alone so I went to the top of the tell and sat and just let my mind drift. As I was sitting there I saw some shepherds at the water hole below me. As I watched I observed one of the shepherds go and gather his sheep. He used his staff to push them along. Then as I was watching another shepherd did a funny little whistle and began walking away. To my amazement I saw many of the sheep at the water stop drinking and began to follow the shepherd. He did not even look back. I asked one of the people at the dig about what happened and he said the first shepherd was an Arab and the second was a Jew. They herd their flocks differently.

John 10:27
My sheep listen to my voice; I know them, and they follow me.

Dan Says:
"You can listen and follow Jesus or be beat into submission by the things of the world."

# Moments of Ministry

# April 17

An individual had donated some money to the jail ministry to allow some prisoners to purchase Christmas presents for their children. We selected some inmates to participate in the program asking them to give us names and ages of their children. My wife Maxine was put in charge of gathering and wrapping the gifts. Needless to say they were wrapped beautifully. We also had bags of food and a children's Bible in every box. When we gave them out to the families it was a great high for us as we saw the eyes light up and joy fills their faces. One stop made was a trailer that had a fence surrounding it. I entered the gate and was halfway to the house when a large mean dog appeared. I dropped the box and just barely made it out. The mother came out of the house grabbed the box and went inside without a word. I learned a lesson; I wanted the glory that truly belonged to the man who gave the money to buy the gifts. He wanted the glory to go to Jesus.

Luke 11:13
If you then, though you are evil, know how to give good gifts to your children, how much more will your Father in heaven give the Holy Spirit to those who ask him!"

Dan Says:
"The Word says all of God's gifts are wonderful, but the best is LOVE."

# Moments of Ministry

# April 18

We were in Israel and having a wonderful time touring all over. We had finished a long day of seeing as many sights as we could. I wanted to go to the pool area at the hotel and take a soak in the hot tub. Maxine was going to have a swim first and then join me. I approached the hot tub and though there were several people in it I saw that there was room for me. When I got in all of a sudden people stopped talking and started to get out. Soon I realized that there was only myself and one other person, I asked what had happened and he explained that it was the cross I was wearing that was the problem. I was astounded that a simple gold cross could have that effect on all those people.

Matthew 16:24
Then Jesus said to his disciples, "Whoever wants to be my disciple must deny themselves and take up their cross and follow me.

Dan Says:
"The cross can be a symbol of fear to those who refuse to believe."

# Moments
## of Ministry

# April 19

My brother's best friend lived with us growing up. He was there for every meal and spent most of his nights with us. He and my brother Jack decided that they would enter the army together. They went through boot camp together and were able to be assigned to the paratrooper division. As it ended up they were separated and Howie was sent to Korea and jumped into the area of the Pusan Reservoir as many U.S. troops were trapped there. We had made my mom his beneficiary of his insurance and we were notified that he was missing in action and presumed dead. We all grieved for a long time. One New Years we were having a party and suddenly the doorbell rang and when we answered there stood Howie. The joy was completely out of hand as we all gathered around and asked what happened. It seemed that he was taken captive but was exchanged later on. Wow what a wonderful new year.

John 5:24
"Very truly I tell you, whoever hears my word and believes him who sent me has eternal life and will not be judged but has crossed over from death to life.

Dan Says:
"All life is in the hands of the Lord He takes away and gives back."

# MOMENTS
## OF MINISTRY

# April 20

There we were standing on the beach at Waikiki holding hands and renewing the wedding vows that we made fifty years earlier. Many people were gathering around and our family was proudly watching the proceedings. The setting was perfect with the white sandy beach the beautiful palm trees and the blue Pacific Ocean. My Grandson Josh was conducting the ceremony and we all were so happy. There was my wife Maxine, with a lei of flowers around her neck, even more beautiful this time than the first. I do not think I was ever more proud to be a man than I was that day. You would think that love would wane after all those years; it was just the opposite our love had grown even greater. Wow!! God knew what He was doing when He gave me Maxine.

Proverbs 31:10
A wife of noble character who can find? She is worth far more than rubies

Dan Says:
"When you get a good woman do not let anything get between you except Jesus."

# MOMENTS
## OF MINISTRY

# April 21

When you are in Athens the must see place is the Acropolis where the Parthenon and other buildings of antiquity are located. For me the greatest place of interest was the Areopagus; which is sometimes called Mars Hill. It was where the apostle Paul went to speak to the intellectuals of the Greek kingdom. It sits next to the great hill of temples and is not too impressive until you get to the edge and look down. There below are the ruins of the old market place below. I got a whole new respect for Paul when I learned that if the Stoics and Philosophers did not like what you had to say you were thrown off the ledge. So when Paul spoke he literally took his life into his hands. How would you like to give a sermon and your life depended on the acceptance.

Acts 17:34
Some of the people became followers of Paul and believed. Among them was Dionysius, a member of the Areopagus, also a woman named Damaris, and a number of others.

Dan Says:
"When you risk it all for Jesus He wins."

# MOMENTS
## OF MINISTRY

# April 22

My partner and I were on plain-clothes patrol in downtown San Francisco on Market Street, when we heard the scream. As we headed toward the sound we saw a young man running with a purse in his hand. My partner simply held out his arm and clotheslined him. A few weeks later we had to go to court to testify against the thief. He had a real bad thing happen to him. He was to appear before a judge who had her purse snatched and she was knocked into a swimming pool. Luckily an officer was passing and was able to rescue her. But since then this judge was very harsh in her sentencing of this type of thief. She did not disappoint us; he got more time than most armed robbers did.

Proverbs 21:15
When justice is done, it brings joy to the righteous but terror to evildoers.

Dan Says:
"Sometimes some things just work out perfectly."

# MOMENTS
## OF MINISTRY

# April 23

When I play golf with Bob it is a wonderful treat. Not only is the fellowship great and the fierce competition stimulating, but there is also the white box. Bob's wife Sue makes cookies to die for and she always sends some in a white box when we play. One day when I arrived at the course and got into Bob's golf cart I did not see a white box. I did not say anything, but Bob must have seen the disappointment on my face. As I was out of the cart hitting a shot, Bob was on the phone; I assumed that it was business as he often took calls while playing. When we got to the fourth hole, Bob walked away from the course to the street and went to his car. I saw him coming back with a big smile, but more importantly a beautiful white box.

> Haggai 1:9
> You expected much, but see, it turned out to be little.

> Dan Says:
> "When you expect much, you get much. God expects it all."

# Moments of Ministry

# April 24

As soon as the plane landed in Seattle all I could think about was breakfast. I had been working at an archeological dig in Israel for the last month. We had been staying at a religious kibbutz in Israel and we had been eating kosher food. The food was good and very healthy but tomatoes and cucumbers for breakfast was not my first choice. Out the door of the airport to a cab stand where we told the driver to take us to a good breakfast place. When we arrived the waitress came to take my order and I said" two eggs over easy and bacon, sausage, and ham". She asked which one I wanted and I replied all three. I think that was the most enjoyable breakfast I ever ate.

Psalm 37:4
Take delight in the Lord, and he will give you the desires of your heart.

Dan Says:
"If only we missed the things of God as much as we miss the things of the world."

# Moments
## of Ministry

# April 25

We were sitting on the corner waiting for the light to change. I looked across the street and two men came out of a tavern, as I was watching I observed one man stab the other and go back inside. I radioed for help and then went to the side door and placed my dog Shelby on alert at the door. I went to the front with a shotgun and waited for help to arrive. One of the men inside had decided to come out the side door. Shelby put on a full mouth bite on the man and he struggled to get back inside. The bar was full of motorcycle types and when we came inside the floor was littered with guns, knives and all kinds of drugs. I carefully looked at each man and could not identify the man who had committed the stabbing. Suddenly a portion of the ceiling came down and we knew where the suspect was. We lifted the dog onto the false ceiling and soon we heard the yelling. The man kicked away the tiles and when he fell to the floor the dog was still attached. He was the suspect. We arrested everyone for murder and disturbing the peace.

Psalm 37:38
But all sinners will be destroyed; there will be no future for the wicked.

Dan Says:
"Like the police dog, God also will seek out evildoers and punish them."

# MOMENTS OF MINISTRY

# April 26

As I was sitting at my desk at the mission the doorman came to me and told me that there was someone who wanted to talk to me. A young man entered in and sat across from me. I asked what the problem was and he reached under his shirt and pulled out a forty-five caliber pistol and laid it on the desk between us. I do not have to tell you that this made me very nervous and I really wanted to reach for it, but was afraid that it might set him off. I tried to stay calm and ask what his problem was. He related to me that he was in school and that his whole family had saved and worked to get him through college and that he was failing in his classes. I asked him what type of work his father did and he said he was a warehouseman. I asked if it was honorable work and he replied it was. I explained that not everyone was meant to be a college graduate, but as long as you tried and did your best that was all anyone could ask of you. We prayed together and I said for him to send his dad to get the weapon I talked to his father and told him that he had to let his son live his own life.

Ephesians 6:4
Fathers, do not exasperate your children; instead, bring them up in the training and instruction of the Lord.

Dan Says:
"Even if we could live our children's life for them, we would just screw it up."

# Moments of Ministry

# April 27

The night that Park Station was bombed I was sent outside the Hall of Justice to look for explosive devices. As I came around the corner of the building I saw a car pull up and a man with a rifle got out and aimed it at the building. I immediately drew my pistol and fired at him... I hit the suspect and he was found later dead in the driveway of a hospital in Oakland. I found out he was a member of a radical group The Weathermen. They sent written threats against my family and me. We lived across the bay in the small town of Mill Valley. Those officers were very diligent in protecting my family and home. They would come by several times a night while I was working. A neighbor became curious and came down the side of our house to see what the police were looking for. My wife heard them and called and every officer in town came red light and siren. The neighbor was stopped questioned and released, and never came near again.

Psalm 116:6
The Lord protects the unwary; when I was brought low, he saved me.

Dan Says:
"The bond among brothers in arms is impossible to break."

# Moments of Ministry

# April 28

We live next door to a family who watches some little girls. They are kind of fun to watch but can be a pest with all their questions. We rescued a Boxer dog and named him after the great fighter John L Sullivan. John, the boxer was playing in the yard and the little girl was in her yard. We have a chain link fence so they could see each other. The little girl was watching as John was playing with our daughter's dog Kona. She called John to the fence and in a very serious tone said "John what is the other dog's name?' I had to laugh, but then I saw the innocence of a child and how easily she could believe. I wish we were all like that sometimes.

1 Corinthians 13:11
When I was a child, I talked like a child, I thought like a child, I reasoned like a child.

Dan Says:
"Think like an adult, but believe like a child."

# Moments of Ministry

# April 29

My friend and I were prospecting for sapphires in the mountains of Montana. We had hit a good hole and were finding a lot of stones and instead of washing the dirt off there we placed them in five gallon buckets to wash at home. We had finished for the day and were eating dinner when I noticed a pink fog closing in from the west. When I told my friend he said "they have that all the time in Chicago". Soon particles of ash were falling all over us and we thought there was a fire near. We gathered our gear and proceeded out of the mountains. When we got into radio range we heard that Mount Saint Helen had erupted. They said all highways were closed and no traffic was allowed. We made our way home by back roads and were relieved to find our families were safe.

Psalm 34:4
I sought the Lord, and he answered me; he delivered me from all my fears.

Dan Says:
"Our greatest fear is the unknown, nice to know where we are going to end up."

# Moments of Ministry

# April 30

It is always an evening of fun when you are with friends from your bowling league. There is one instance when the fun goes away and all that remains is pressure. It is when you bowl a perfect three hundred game. I remember my first, the first three strikes are called a turkey, and then one more is a four-bagger. When the fifth and sixth strike comes, you began to think possibly you just might do it. You make the seventh and eighth strike and people move away from you and do not talk anymore. My ninth was a perfect hit and people from all over the lanes were gathering around to see if it was going to happen. The last frame my legs were shaking and I was sweating. The first ball in the tenth went into the pocket just perfect, the second was the worst strike I have ever seen the pins went down, but it was pure luck. I took a deep breath and released the last ball it went into the pocket like it had eyes. The place erupted and I was both elated and relieved. But bowling was never the same afterward; you only bowl your first three hundred once.

John 15:11
I have told you this so that my joy may be in you and that your joy may be complete.

Dan Says:
"If only we sought after the things of God like we do the things of the world."

# Moments of Ministry

# May 1

Being brand new in ministry and in my forties I was nervous coming to candidate at my first church. I had a good friend who recommended me to the congregation. After I delivered my first sermon and was driving home, I asked my friend how I had done. He said I managed to insult everyone in the small congregation. I asked how I will know if they like me. He said they would not come back if they do not like you. The next Sunday my wife and I came to church early and waited for people to arrive. Twenty minutes after the service was supposed to start I said to Maxine lets go get a donut. After we had finished our donuts we were heading home. As we passed the church we saw many cars in the lot. We stopped and then it dawned on us Daylight Savings had started.

Psalm 103:5
…who satisfies your desires with good things so that your youth is renewed like the eagle's.

Dan Says:
"If you do what you think God wants, God will not disappoint."

# Moments of Ministry

# May 2

We were still in the police academy when Chinese New Year arrived. We were to be assigned to direct traffic at the parade. There were two of us on each corner and our job was to keep traffic moving. A fight had started out right in front of us so I went to try and restore order. Instead the suspect decided that he wanted to fight. When help showed up I had one man in handcuffs and another on the ground. A paddy wagon showed up and we placed the suspects inside. I then asked an officer what was next and he said to make a report. I had no idea what he was talking about so I asked him. He gave me a number to call and said just tell them what happened. I called the number and a transcriptionist said when you finish the report just whistle. I said "Lynch stuck two guys in the wagon" and then whistled. The following Monday at the academy I was the butt of many jokes and that report followed me my whole career.

1 Timothy 1:7
They want to be teachers of the law, but they do not know what they are talking about or what they so confidently affirm.

Dan Says:
"Take the time to get all the information before taking action."

# Moments
## of Ministry

# May 3

All of us were looking forward to observing all the aquatic life on the Kona whale watching cruise. We went aboard and all found places that would give us unobstructed views to watch all the whales and other sea life. After an hour or so the skipper of the boat came on the loudspeaker to declare that this was the worst day he and his crew had ever experienced for watching sea life. After more false alarms and a couple of hours later the skipper said he would take us back to shore, and we could have another day on the boat for free. Later that same day we were at our condo when we heard many sirens go off and then we were advised to get into our auto and seek higher ground. We went to a parking lot and spent the night there, until the tsunami warning was lifted. I guess the sea life did not have to hear a warning to seek deeper water.

>Psalm 3:8
>From the Lord comes deliverance.

Dan Says:
"If He cares for the fish in the sea, how much more will He care for you."

# Moments of Ministry

# May 4

During the 1988 intifada in Israel I got the bright idea to go into the Arab Quarter of the old city. There was a great deal of unrest in the city of Jerusalem and many of the shops in the old city would not open. We were walking through the old city when a young man approached Maxine and I. He said that he would open his shop for us alone and give us great bargains. We agreed to go to his shop and he did let us in a side door. As soon as we entered I knew we had made a very big mistake. Sitting about there were five young Arab men who did not look friendly at all. They asked what kind of work I did and I told them I was a policeman. We then left the shop and found ourselves in a deserted section of the old city. The young men began to follow us so I headed for the Jewish quarter, when we got there I realized that it was Sabbath and everything was closed. Suddenly we came to a plaza and there was a taxi, we jumped in and asked to be taken to our hotel. The driver took us through a gate and down some stairs and made an impossible turn and then we were out of the old city. I believe to this day that the cab driver was an angel of God who saved us.

Psalm 34:4
I sought the Lord, and he answered me; he delivered me from all my fears.

Dan Says:
"No matter how stupid you are He will still watch over you in times of trouble."

# Moments
## of Ministry

# May 5

They were bringing in a four masted schooner to put on display down on fisherman's wharf. The name of the ship was the Balcutha and my father said that we had to see it. I was not too excited to go see an old sailing ship but my dad said it was important so off we went. When we arrived at the ship we paid the entrance fee and went aboard. There was a man who was on the ship to make sure no one would steal anything. My father went to him and asked if we could go below and he said absolutely not. My dad then talked to him alone and then the man said all right we could go below. My dad took me to the berthing area and as we walked around he said to follow him. We came to some bunk beds and my father said look at this. I looked at the bottom of the upper bunk and there carved into the wood was my father's name. He then told me stories of when he sailed around the cape in this vessel from Africa to San Francisco. I saw my dad in a new light after that.

Deuteronomy 6:9
Write them on the doorframes of your houses and on your gates.

Dan Says:
"What you do not tell your children, they will never know."

# Moments of Ministry

# May 6

I talked to everyone I knew trying to get a chance to play golf at the exclusive Black Rock Golf Course. For several years I would try but I did not know any members who could get me a time to play. Then one day a friend who attended one of my Bible studies came to me and said Dan you are going to play Black Rock. Boy was I excited I asked how he managed to got the invite and he said he was going to play a concert there and part of the contract was that I would get to play the course. I was overjoyed at the chance to play. When we got our foursome together we went up to play the course. The clubhouse was very elegant and I was very impressed. But when we played the course I found that I did not like it at all. The holes were too long and the course was very hard to play. We finished the game and I bought the shirt so all would know I played the course. But whole experience left me wondering. If we do not all have expectations that are not as important as we think.

John 2:17
The world and its desires pass away, but whoever does the will of God lives forever.

Dan Says:
"When we get what we always want sometimes it is not all that wonderful."

# Moments of Ministry

# May 7

I had returned home from boot camp and was eating dinner with the family. It was good to sit at the table with mom and dad and sister. And enjoy each other's company. At boot camp I went through with an all Alabama company. There was one other fellow who was not from the south and we became buddies. He was the only guy I could understand beside the drill instructor. The men from Alabama talked so slow that I forgot the first word by the time they said the third one. It was frustrating and annoying to be around them for any length of time. One day one of the southern boys came to me and said if you do not slow down your talking no one will ever understand you. I responded as slowly as I could "shut up and go away'. Now at dinner at home with the family I was having a terrible time understanding my own family because they were talking way too fast.

James 4:1
What causes fights and quarrels among you? Don't they come from your desires that battle within you?

Dan Says:
"By exposure you can become the very thing you despise, stay away from evil."


# MOMENTS
## OF MINISTRY

# May 8

There is an old guy at our church that has a small ranch and raises animals for slaughter. He feeds his animals old bread and donuts and other food that would otherwise be thrown away. I was walking with him around his place one day and he was showing me his operation. He kills then skins and butchers the meat in his own butcher shop. While we were walking around we came upon a mother duck and twelve little ducks following behind her. They were a special breed he had for some people in Seattle. When I looked at all those little ducks I asked how the mother duck could feed them all, as there were too many for breast-feeding. I thought he would fall over laughing when he heard that question. He said how could you be so dumb? I told him I grew up in San Francisco and had never been on a farm. If an animal did not sit when I told it to then I didn't know anything about it.

Ecclesiastes 9:7
Go, eat your food with gladness, and drink your wine with a joyful heart, for God has already approved what you do.

Dan Says:
"We each have our place in God's plan. Do yours with respect for others."

# Moments of Ministry

# May 9

It was one of those days when everything was a downer. I was the Chaplain at the jail and was exhausted from all the woes I had been presented with that day. Even the guards were in sour moods and wanted to talk about all that was bothering them. I finally decided to get out of there and go get a haircut. When I got into the barber chair I just wanted to be left alone, but the barber continued to ask questions all leading to an evangelism opportunity, but I just wanted him to shut up! I paid for the haircut and started back to the jail when the Holy Spirit just slammed me. I knew I had to go back. I entered the shop and another man was having his haircut. The barber was looking at me wondering what I was doing back there. I got into the chair and the barber asked what I wanted and I said just a trim. I finally explained to the man that I was a preacher and I did not respond correctly to his questions. He laughed and said that was all right he was a Christian and he understood. Then He said "I am going to charge you for this haircut so you will remember". He did and I do.

Ephesians 5:15-16
Be very careful, then, how you live—not as unwise but as wise, making the most of every opportunity, because the days are evil.

Dan Says:
"When nobody is looking be the man God wants you to be."

# MOMENTS OF MINISTRY

# May 10

Everyone had left the bus and started up to the top of the tel in Zippora. I was alone with Yoel the bus driver and we began to talk seriously about Jesus. He said that he was listening as I spoke throughout the tour and he had some questions. We talked and I answered his questions as best I could and he said he wanted to think about what I had said. I left him to think and began to walk and pray as we waited for the guide and people to come back to the bus. When we were all seated in the bus and everyone counted, Yoel stood up in front of everyone and announced that he was now a Christian. The whole bus erupted in applause and smiles were everywhere. I later talked to Yoel and made sure that he understood what he was doing. We became good friends and stayed in contact for many years.

Matthew 28:19
Therefore go and make disciples of all nations, baptizing them in the name of the Father and of the Son and of the Holy Spirit,

Dan Says:
"You never know who is listening when you talk about Jesus."

# Moments
## of Ministry

# May 11

We had been working at the archeological site at Lachish and were staying at a religious kibbutz in Israel. The food is very healthy in the kibbutz but I had heard from one of the volunteers that there was a donut shop in Jerusalem. When I found that out all I could think of was donuts. You do know that donuts are soul food for a retired policeman. Finally Friday came and we had to be off the kibbutz as we were not Jewish. So we set off for Jerusalem and got ourselves a hotel room. I was rooming with another pastor and he also wanted a donut in the worst way. When I came out of the shower I heard John let out a cry of despair. I ran into the room and John showed me the front page of the Jerusalem Post newspaper. There on the page was a photo of a bombing in Jerusalem. You guessed it the American Donut Shop. My donuts were scattered all over the street. Oh what disappointment I felt.

1 John 2:17
The world and its desires pass away, but whoever does the will of God lives forever.

Dan Says:
"We all will live with disappointment in our lives, but we can choose to remember the joy."

# MOMENTS
## OF MINISTRY

# May 12

When you are standing in formation at a large disturbance the crowd shouts insults and sometimes even throws things at you. I have been hit with bags of feces, rocks, and even pool balls. Still we must remain in formation, but our minds are only listening for the horn. When the officer in charge decides that it is time to disperse the crowd he presses a button on his bullhorn and a loud beep is heard. That is our signal to advance and the standing and taking all of the abuse is over and we can advance and do our job we were trained for. The waiting is hard, but when we are released everything we go through is worth it.

Ecclesiastes 3:1
There is a time for everything, and a season for every activity under the heavens:

Dan Says:
"Waiting is hard, but sometimes worth the wait."

# Moments of Ministry

# May 13

The sergeant had come to my house to pick me up to play golf. I invited him in the house and said I would be right back, as I had to change clothes. He was a nice guy and I had just come on to his team and we were getting to know each other. As I was in the bedroom I heard a great commotion in the dining room, there was much yelling and I could not imagine what was going on. When I came into the room there was Chris standing on my dining room table. I asked what was going on and he said that my dog, Valiant, had just come up to him and began to show his teeth, then he emitted the meanest growl he had ever heard. Chris said to me "If dogs take on the personality of their owners that I was a welcome member of the team." I would be able to keep the team in check.

Titus 1:9
He must hold firmly to the trustworthy message as it has been taught, so that he can encourage others by sound doctrine and refute those who oppose it.

Dan Says:
"Each man in a team must do his job to have an effective mission accomplished."

# MOMENTS OF MINISTRY

# May 14

We were sitting on the senior's bench at lunchtime at our high school when Ray my best friend showed me a picture of a girl. I was in love as soon as I saw that photo; she was a blond and was wearing shorts. Wow!!! All I could think of was to have Ray introduce me to her. He said he did not know her and I was crushed. He did say that she was a friend of his girl friend so joy was back in my heart again. When I met Maxine I was unable to even talk she was more beautiful in person than in the picture. We did arrange a double date and went out together. We started dating and eventually got married. Today fifty-seven years later she is still the most beautiful woman I have ever seen.

Song of Songs 1:15
How beautiful you are, my darling! Oh, how beautiful! Your eyes are doves.

Dan Says:
"When you find the one let nothing stand in your way of getting her."

# Moments of Ministry

# May 15

I was still at the Bible College and taking every opportunity to preach at Old folk's homes, small churches and any other venue that I could dig up. I remember once I had prepared a sermon that went on and on. I was sure that the audience was enthralled with all of my great words of wisdom. You really know when you put your whole heart and mind into a sermon and it all comes together. Finally I finished my masterpiece and accepted all the platitudes of my audience who I am sure were just overjoyed that I had finally finished. We got into the car and on the way home I said to my wife "I wonder how many really great preachers there are?' Her reply was classic" one less than you think". I really needed that and have not forgotten her wise statement.

Proverbs 16:18
Pride goes before destruction, a haughty spirit before a fall.

Dan Says:
"The truth from someone who loves you is worth more than flattery from strangers."

# Moments
## of Ministry

# May 16

I have many photos on the wall in my office some are self-explanatory and some have meaning only for me. One of my favorites is a photo that I took in Jerusalem. The picture is of a girl with long black hair looking in the window of a shop that had all kind of girly things. The thing that makes this photo different is what she is wearing; an army uniform and also slung over her shoulder is an Uzi machine gun. The dramatic difference in the whole scene is fascinating to me. It must be hard for a people to live like this at war her whole life and still a young woman who wants the nicer things in life. Though she did not know it my heart went out to her and I pray that someday the young in Israel will just be able to enjoy their youth.

Psalm 122:6-7
Pray for the peace of Jerusalem: "May those who love you be secure. May there be peace within your walls and security within your citadels."

Dan Says:
"War is always started by the old and fought by the young."

# MOMENTS OF MINISTRY

# May 17

When you walked the Embarcadero beat you knew that the beat sergeant trusted you. It was the toughest beat in the southern police district being on the docks where the longshoremen were enjoying their off time from unloading ships. The bars in the district were not for the tourist or the faint of heart. I can remember when I was with the sergeant on the beat and someone came up to us and said "Spider was at it again". The sergeant said for me to go into the Hot Spot and take care of the problem. I entered the bar and everyone was looking at a guy standing at the end of the bar holding a man in a headlock. I asked him to let the man go and he said sure. I then requested that he join me outside the bar. When we hit the sidewalk all of a sudden this man took a fighters stance and told me he was about to kick my *&^. I told him if he would come quietly that the next time I saw him on the beat I would buy him a beer. He agreed and went easily into the Paddy Wagon. The sergeant then told me that the man was Spider Webb a world contender in the boxing ring, and no one had ever arrested him alone. The boss said this is now your beat. Enjoy!

James 1:19
My dear brothers and sisters, take note of this: Everyone should be quick to listen, slow to speak and slow to become angry, because human anger does not produce the righteousness that God desires.

Dan Says:
"Smarter is way better than tougher, to get by in this world."

# Moments
## of Ministry

# May 18

I had brought home a man from the mission to live with us. He was trying hard to fit in and we were just getting to know each other and were working hard at making this adjustment to both our lives. Christmas morning and we had opened all of our presents and Mike jumped right up to clean everything. We had a wood stove so he put in all the wrapping paper and boxes to burn. As I gathered my presents to put them in my room I found that a tie that Maxine gave me was missing. We searched high and low to no avail. The only conclusion was that the tie went into the wood stove. Mike was devastated and completely crushed. When we explained it was only a tie and we were not upset he calmed down and said if that had happened in his home there would be screaming forever.

Philippians 3:13-14
Forgetting what is behind and straining toward what is ahead, 14 I press on toward the goal to win the prize for which God has called me heavenward in Christ Jesus.

Dan Says:
"Stuff happens."

# Moments
## of Ministry

# May 19

I had just gotten a new boat and was trying to master all the things that came with boat ownership. One of the most difficult things to accomplish was the backing up to put the boat into the water. I had taken my grandson Josh out to fish and we were attempting to launch the boat. As I was backing up I asked Josh how I was doing. His reply was priceless he said, "If you are trying to hit the water not so good". After I stopped laughing I said, "instead of being a smart aleck maybe you could stand in front of the truck and direct me into the water".

2 Timothy 4:5
But you, keep your head in all situations, endure hardship, do the work of an evangelist, discharge all the duties of your ministry.

Dan Says:
"A man who can laugh in all his frustrations will be a joy to be around."

# MOMENTS OF MINISTRY

# May 20

A whole group of us went over to a friend's house for an evening of fun and fellowship. Several of us began to play cards and were having a great time when the hostess brought out some snacks. She placed by my elbow a big bowl of dried banana chips and some hot tea. As the evening wore on I ate the whole bowl of chips and downed it with several cups of hot tea. When I arrived home my stomach swelled to about twice the normal size and really began to hurt. All my wife could do is laugh because she knew that nature would take its course and all would come out fine. I know now there is too much of a good thing.

Romans 14:15
If your brother or sister is distressed because of what you eat, you are no longer acting in love.

Dan Says:
"Learn to enjoy the fellowship more than the food."

# Moments of Ministry

# May 21

We were in London and we had gone down a side street to a fish and chips restaurant. We felt we must have fish and chips in London because that is what all the locals do. As we ordered at the counter I saw the different types of fish so I decided to experiment and ordered skate. My wife when asked if she wanted pea mash said that she would give it a try. Let me tell you that skate is a bunch of bones with very little meat on them and what was there tasted terrible. Maxine had the pea mash and it was just as it sounds a bunch of peas mashed, not very tasty. We went out disappointed and about a block later I saw a sign in the window that said this store sells pasties. Well joy reigned in London, as I was overjoyed to find my favorite food in the world.

Acts 8:8
So there was great joy in that city.

Dan Says:
"Sorrow does not have to last. Joy can be just around the corner."

# Moments of Ministry

# May 22

I was standing behind the counter at the motel waiting to be robbed. An informant had told us that this motel was to be held up tonight. My partner was in the room behind me with a shotgun if he was needed. I was hoping that the hold up man was not high on some drug that would make him mean. Soon the wait was over. I saw him through the glass window pull his gun from under his jacket. He charged at the counter with the gun in front and without a word began to shoot. I ducked and my partner came out from in back firing his gun and I stood and shot several times with mine. The robber went down and so did we. He was hit and we were hiding behind the counter. After a while we came out and he was down and not conscious. Even knowing what could happen did not prepare us for the fear we experienced.

2 Peter 3:10
But the day of the Lord will come like a thief.

Dan Says:
"Even knowing does not take away the great fear of your destruction."

# MOMENTS
## OF MINISTRY

# May 23

It was at a department meeting that I was honored for fifty years in law enforcement. My granddaughter was a dispatcher at Post Falls Police Department, she and the Chief arranged the program. I was sitting there minding my own business when the Chief called me forward and had me watch a slide show of all of my medals of valor and my history as a Chaplain. I was very touched by it all and then they awarded me a beautiful plaque that said some very nice things. I was both humbled and proud at the same time. It was very rewarding to be appreciated by the people with whom you work. The law enforcement community is not much into awards so I was very happy to so see that my volunteer work was making a difference.

Romans 13:4
For the one in authority is God's servant for your good. But if you do wrong, be afraid, for rulers do not bear the sword for no reason. They are God's servants, agents of wrath to bring punishment on the wrongdoer.

Dan Says:
"Responding to God's call is not even work it is a life of joy."

# Moments of Ministry

# May 24

My wife and I were driving our rented car in Israel and while on a road we were stopped to let a flock of sheep cross the road. As we were watching I noticed that one of the shepherds was riding a donkey and was in full Arab dress except he had a pair of Nike tennis shoes with the Nike swoosh. As we traveled along we began to notice the mixing of the ancient with the modern. We passed a Bedouin encampment and next to the tent was a beautiful Mercedes parked. When I showed my wife she said look at the television antenna sticking out of the roof of the tent. In the Mideast there is a strange mixture of old and new, where east and west come together in the culture. We loved to go to Israel and it was sad to see the changes as we went back year after year.

1 John 3:7
Dear children, do not let anyone lead you astray. The one who does what is right is righteous, just as he is righteous.

Dan Says:
"I must be getting old I do not think that new is always better."

# MOMENTS
## OF MINISTRY

# May 25

We got a new dog she was a lab, her name was Fuzzy and she was as cute as could be. My next-door neighbor also had a lab named Spud. Spud was a wonderful hunter and we often took him bird hunting. Once we decided it was time for Fuzzy to learn to hunt so we took her along for some pheasant hunting. Almost as soon as we got out of the truck at a cornfield Spud kicked up a bird for us. We shot the bird and cut off the wing for Fuzzy to smell and play with. As we were walking down a row of corn Fuzzy suddenly took off. I called and called and searched for her everywhere. I was worried about what would happen to me when I came home without Fuzzy. Then all my worries were over, here came Fuzzy with a live pheasant in her mouth. She was very proud and I was very relieved. My wife put an end to hunting when one time I brought her home full of mud especially between her toes. She lived with us for many years and gave the whole family great pleasure.

James 3:7-8
All kinds of animals, birds, reptiles and sea creatures are being tamed and have been tamed by mankind, but no human being can tame the tongue. It is a restless evil, full of deadly poison.

Dan Says:
"If animals can be taught the right way, it should be easy for us to learn also."

# Moments of Ministry

# May 26

Sitting in a coat outlet waiting for my wife and daughters to try on coats was taking forever. Luckily there were some chairs in the front of the store and I sat in one of them. There was a man sitting next to me and I decided to strike up a conversation with him. As we talked I noticed how sad he was and then he told me what had happened. His teenage daughter was riding a horse and it fell and somehow rolled over her and she died. I told him how sorry I was and asked if she was a Christian, he replied that she was and used to talk to him about the Lord. After talking a bit longer I asked him if he ever wanted to see his daughter again and he said yes. I explained about heaven and how salvation works and he joyfully accepted the Lord. I told him to go to his daughter's church and tell them what he had done and they would help him with more understanding.

1 Peter 3:15
But in your hearts revere Christ as Lord. Always be prepared to give an answer to everyone who asks you to give the reason for the hope that you have.

Dan Says:
"Always pray that God will use you for His glory."

# Moments of Ministry

# May 27

I got a call to go to mission station right away. I wondered what they would want with me as I was patrolling in another district. When I got to the station the desk sergeant told me that they had my father in custody in the station cell. I asked what the charge was and he said assault. I went back to the cell and asked my dad what happened and he explained that he had just cashed hi pay check and was walking home when two young toughs told him to hand over his money. Instead he backed up a stairway and when they came at him he kicked them down the stairs. A woman was passing by and called the police and when they arrived she insisted that my dad be arrested. I talked to the captain and he called the woman and told her she could be sued for false arrest. She immediately dropped the charges and I was able to drive my dad home.

Psalm 106:3
Blessed are those who act justly, who always do what is right.

Dan Says:
"Sometimes God uses circumstances to punish the evil doers."

# MOMENTS
## OF MINISTRY

# May 28

I had gone into the dealership to buy a used car. The salesman was a friend from church and I wanted to help him get a sale. While looking over the lots, all of a sudden he received a call. It seems that a beautiful auto with low mileage had just been traded in and was just what I wanted. We struck a deal and as we were walking back to the finance department the owner of the dealership came up to us. My friend introduced my wife and I to the owner who asked me if I was the preacher who had spoken at church last weekend. I said I was and he said to the salesman to give me a thousand dollar discount. I was really surprised and then I told him I was preaching next week also. He laughed and said keep up the good work.

James 1:17
Every good and perfect gift is from above, coming down from the Father of the heavenly lights, who does not change like shifting shadows.

Dan Says:
"Blessings come in many ways and in many forms."

# Moments
## of Ministry

# May 29

Going to Bible school in my late forties was an adventure for me. When I went to check out the school I noticed that I was older than most of the professors. I was very nervous about going with all the young students so I had my wife join me. They all treated us with much respect especially my wife. However after a short time they began to have fun with me. They all called me the old geezer, but they were doing it in a fun way. They loved to sit and hear all about my adventures in the navy and the police force. I even had the chance to be the soccer coach for the school team. After a while I kind of became the father confessor of my class. I got a lot of practice to sharpen my skills as a pastor while I was still in school. Upon graduation my wife and I went to our car and it was decorated with the words congratulation you old geezer. That really was the best thing that could have happened.

I Timothy 5:17
The elders who direct the affairs of the church well are worthy of double honor, especially those whose work is preaching and teaching.

Dan Says:
"Sometimes you are an elder without seeking the office."

# MOMENTS OF MINISTRY

# May 30

There walking down the street in Jerusalem were four young girls giggling and laughing with each other. The thing that made this different was the dress of the girls. Two of them were in school uniforms of some sort with white blouses and blue skirts. The other two were in full Arab dress with dresses that came to the ground and their heads were covered so no hair was showing. As they walked and joked and had fun with each other I saw that there was an opportunity for people of different faiths to get along and enjoy the differences between them. It is my fervent prayer that like these girls that all the people of Israel can find common ground to come together and not only have peace, but really enjoy their differences.

2 Peter 3:14
So then, dear friends, since you are looking forward to this, make every effort to be found spotless, blameless and at peace with him.

Dan Says:
"The young have to be taught to hate, we are all born with the love of God."

# Moments
## of Ministry

# May 31

We were pulling the boat out of the water; and after much trouble I managed to get the boat on the trailer. As I pulled forward there was a huge crash and as I looked back there was my boat standing on its back end. The rope that was attached to the trailer had broken and the boat had fallen off the back of the trailer. As I stood in disbelief a man who was standing on the dock said to me "your trouble is that the rope parted". Now my first instinct was to run over and throw him off the dock. My grandson knowing my temper immediately said, "I didn't mean it grandpa", and then turned his back. I could see his shoulders moving as he laughed at my fury. The man at the dock came over and said he could help me get the boat on the trailer. He pulled his truck down and used a winch to get my boat settled on the trailer. I thanked him and was glad that I had held my temper.

Psalm 30:5
For his anger lasts only a moment, but his favor lasts a lifetime;

Dan Says:
"A temper that is lost is not easily found."

# Moments
## of Ministry

# June 1

We all heard the alarm go off; as we raced down to the waters edge everyone was hoping that the rod that was sounding the alarm was his. I was delighted to see my rod bent and jumping with a sure sign that a fish was on. As the others, disappointed, walked back to camp I brought the nice fat trout into shore and cleaned it. Now this is the way to fish I was thinking to myself. My next-door neighbor had developed the fish alarm and we all used it. It was a bicycle horn attached to a metal stake. When a fish took the bait and tried to get away, the horn sounded. It made it fun as we could play cards or just sit in camp and talk and still fish. We did manage to do more than one thing at a time. I used that knowledge to help me through life to accomplish many things. I could drive the car to work and learn a foreign language at the same time. I also used it in many other ways as well. What a great lesson to learn.

James 1:14
but each person is tempted when they are dragged away by their own evil desire and enticed.

Dan Says:
"When it is too good to be true, it usually is."

# MOMENTS
## OF MINISTRY

# June 2

We heard a whining at our front door and went to investigate upon opening the door we found a little black and white puppy. It was well below freezing so we brought him in and immediately fell in love with him. My daughter Colleen was the one to name him and she selected the name Bozo, well he sure lived up to his name. The entire time we had him, which was several years; his only thought was to run away. One time he ran away and the animal control officer picked him up and took him to the animal shelter. My wife went to pay the fine and get him released from the shelter. After paying the fine she went with the shelter worker to get Bozo and when she called him to come out of the kennel he would not come. The shelter worker asked if she was sure that it was her dog. She had to explain that he was very independent and did not mind us very well. We loved and cared for him anyway right up to the end of his life.

1 Thessalonians 5:15
Make sure that nobody pays back wrong for wrong, but always strive to do what is good for each other and for everyone else.

Dan Says:
"How others treat you does not relieve you of the responsibility to treat them with respect."

# Moments
## of Ministry

# June 3

The seven-pointed star, the badge for the San Francisco Police Department, was silver and only weighed a few ounces, but when they pinned it on me it seemed very heavy because of the responsibility that came with it. It took many weeks at the academy and a tremendous amount of training both mental and physical to earn the right to wear that symbol of authority. I was very proud to be able to wear that star on my uniform and was thinking how wonderful I was. Then I heard the speech at our graduation ceremony that explained how that badge worked. The sergeant said it was not us but that symbol that made us law enforcers. He said no matter who wore that symbol they had all the authority of the law behind them. The power was in the badge not the individual who happened to be wearing it. I know now that it is the same with a cross that some wear it is not the cross, but what that symbol represents.

Luke 9:23
Then he said to them all: "Whoever wants to be my disciple must deny themselves and take up their cross daily and follow me.

Dan Says:
"Remember that it was not a symbol that Our Lord hung on but a real instrument of torture."

# Moments
## of Ministry

# June 4

Imagine when my response to the Holy Spirit was, "You have got to be kidding"? It was as though He was standing in line with me and speaking very clearly to my heart. I continued to hear the same message, as the line grew shorter. My wife had asked me to go to the store on Thanksgiving Day to get a can of peas for dinner because my new son in law liked them. There was only one clerk at the register and the line was long. And now the Holy Spirit said to me "tell the clerk about Jesus". I tried to dismiss the thought, but it was getting more urgent as I drew nearer to her register. I looked about and the line was getting even longer and I was getting panicked. Finally I got to the front of the line with my one can of peas and said," God wants me to talk to you". To my surprise she said that she would get a break in five minutes and meet me at the coffee counter. God moved in her life that day and she accepted Him. And I learned a valuable lesson myself.

2 Timothy 2:15
Do your best to present yourself to God as one approved, a worker who does not need to be ashamed and who correctly handles the word of truth.

Dan Says:
"God can use anybody anytime to accomplish His will."

# Moments of Ministry

# June 5

Due to injuries that I received on the job I was placed on disability leave and had to stay home from work. My wife worked and so I began to do some household chores. I started to watch the cooking shows on television and fancied my self to be a gourmet chef. Some of the meals were pretty good and then there were the others, total flops that even the dog would not consume. Coming from a family who did not have much I hated to waste food, so I would keep all the leftovers from the week and Friday would put it all in one pot and serve it. It was a real mess as I could have soup and corned beef in the same pot with whatever else I could find. My wife finally told me some time later that she made sure to have a big lunch every Friday and the kids also would want to eat at their friend's house every Friday. Looking back I could not blame them.

1 Corinthians 10:31
So whether you eat or drink or whatever you do, do it all for the glory of God.

Dan Says:
"There really is food that those starving kids in China would not eat."

# Moments
## of Ministry

# June 6

I walked out to the back porch with the man while an officer interviewed his wife. In all my years in law enforcement I had never seen a woman beat as badly as this one. I was struggling with what I could say to this individual. He looked at me with a smug smile on his face saying that there was nothing I could do. I then proceed to explain to him that if I was ever called back to this house for a domestic violence report that I would bring a baseball bat and beat him senseless and nobody would believe that a sweet old preacher would do such a thing. He looked at me to see if I was joking and realized I was serious. We had the woman sent to the hospital and another officer took the man to jail to be booked. When I got into the police car with the officer who was on the call he looked at me and said "that was the best sermon he had ever heard". Though I was wrong it turned out for good because all the officers loved what they had heard about me.

Romans 8:28
And we know that in all things God works for the good of those who love him, who have been called according to his purpose.

Dan Says:
"A little fear can be a good thing if the fear is a fear of God."

# Moments of Ministry

# June 7

My father was working the mines in the gold country of California and he was quite a drinker and when he drank he liked to fight. So it was only natural that on one Saturday night he went out and got to drinking and found himself in a fight. The judge Monday morning gave him thirty days in jail. My mother realized that it would be difficult to survive as a family with dad in jail, so she went late at night and set the jail on fire. All the prisoners were released and my father went back to work. He used to say what if the fire department did not let him out what would have happened. Mom said she would have to find a new husband and certainly not an Irish one. My dad said they should have named the new sheriffs office and jail after my mother.

1 Corinthians 8:9
Be careful, however, that the exercise of your rights does not become a stumbling block to the weak.

Dan Says:
"There is a correct way to accomplish what you need to do, so prayer should be first thing you do."

# MOMENTS
## OF MINISTRY

# June 8

We entered the London museum and the first thing I wanted to see were the Katydid Statues that were removed from Athens. I went to the mid-east section of the museum and looked everywhere for them and could not find them. I finally asked a guard where they were to be found and he told me that they were probably stored in the basement. I could not believe that something as important as that would not be on display. I then went to the information booth and asked for a list of antiquities that were not on display. The attendant said that there were thousands of articles in storage that would never be displayed. I asked why they continued to keep them and she said because we own them. How sad that historical objects that belong to another country should be stored in a basement of a museum in distant land.

Matthew 6:19
"Do not store up for yourselves treasures on earth, where moths and vermin destroy, and where thieves break in and steal."

Dan Says:
"What is your is yours what is someone else's is theirs, but it all belongs to God."

# MOMENTS
## OF MINISTRY

# June 9

It finally arrived and in six different boxes, this was going to be some project. My friend Sam and I had decided on a winter project we were going to build grandfather clocks. My wife looked at all the parts and said "Honey I love you, but you will never get a clock out of that mess". We followed the directions and things began to take shape. I wanted to take some shortcuts but Sam would talk me out of it. He said just follow the directions and all will come out all right. We would carefully do exactly as Sam told me to and before long a grandfather clock took shape. The first thing you see coming into our front door is that beautiful grandfather clock.

Proverbs 12:15
The way of fools seems right to them, but the wise listen to advice.

Dan Says:
"We have the best book of instructions, the Bible."

# Moments of Ministry

# June 10

I found myself unable to control my drinking. I would get started and just could not stop myself. It really hurt my marriage and my family life and my work was suffering also. I knew that I had a serious problem and was unable to stop. I finally turned myself in to the captain and he said he would get me help. I was sent to dry out at a detox center in Santa Rosa and was the most ashamed I had ever been. While I was in detox I cried out to the Lord and said if He was truly there he should take over my life as it was out of control. Well I lay down to sleep and slept for eight hours straight, no dreams no problems. I awoke refreshed and knew I was different. But how do I tell people what happened when they do not realize, God had been faithful and protected me for several years until the day I heard the Gospel and realized what had happened to me. I knew that I had to get busy for God as soon as I knew what happened.

Proverbs 13:15
Good judgment wins favor, but the way of the unfaithful leads to their destruction.

Dan Says:
"God is great to us even when we do not acknowledge who He is."

# Moments of Ministry

# June 11

We had left the kibbutz for the weekend and were trying to get to Jerusalem. It was no use we were hopelessly lost and could not find our way. I spotted a police car standing on the side of the road and we stopped. John got out asking directions and as I looked through the windshield I could see he was unable to communicate with the officer. I got out the phrase book and looked up how to ask where Jerusalem was. I walked up to the officer and said "effo ha Jerusalem?' he smiled and went on to tell me exactly how to get to our destination. The only problem was he told me in Hebrew, I smiled and we walked back to the car and John said "Where now?" I replied "I have not the slightest idea."

Luke 19:10
For the Son of Man came to seek and to save the lost.

Dan Says:
"We can have the right information and still not have any understanding at all."

# Moments
## of Ministry

# June 12

I heard the scuffle in the other room and left where I was searching and went to see what was happening. There in the middle of the room was my partner and the suspect going around and around. Then I saw the suspect had my partner's gun and was trying to pull the trigger. My partner had a hold of the cylinder and the gun would not fire. I attempted to get a shot, but they continued to circle around. I finally put my gun away and hit the suspect in the head with my flashlight to no avail. I tried to get him away from my partner but he would not let go of the revolver. I jumped up on his back and put him into a chokehold and after a short while he finally passed out. We handcuffed him and called for transportation to the hospital before booking him into jail. My partner had strained the muscles in his arm so badly that he was off for a week.

Psalm 38:22
Come quickly to help me, my Lord and my Savior.

Dan Says:
"When someone you care for is in danger you want to help. There is a whole world out there in danger of going to hell."

# Moments of Ministry

# June 13

We went to the home of a wealthy Japanese businessman to take a report of some stolen fish. These fish were called koi and were very rare and worth a lot of money. As my partner was taking the report I was wandering the garden when I spotted some small trees. I could not believe my eyes there in front of me was an apple tree with apples on it and it was six inches high. There were a whole bunch of these tiny trees all over the garden. When the report was finished I asked the gardener about these trees. He said they were Bonsai trees and were several years old. He saw my interest and said I could come to his place and see more of them. I went after work and he showed me how they were kept so small, they did not cut the tops of them but trimmed the roots. I purchased a few and brought them home and wanted to have a new hobby. Set in a special place near the fence so they got the best sunlight my trees were put on a special stand. I came home the next day and the dog next door had reached over the fence and destroyed every one of my trees.

2 John 1:8
Watch out that you do not lose what we have worked for, but that you may be rewarded fully.

Dan Says:
"Like Bonsai trees, we Christians can be kept small if we allow our roots to be trimmed by the world."

# Moments of Ministry

# June 14

The poor fellow that I had run into was trying to figure out what was happening at the scene of the accident. There was no doubt as to who was at fault I had attempted to dart between two cars to get to a rest room by the skate park. I had had breakfast and was on the way home when I had a sudden call of nature. I had to go and I mean I had to go now, so I tried to get relief immediately. Well I misjudged and the man in the car hit the rear of my truck. I jumped out and ran to the toilet explaining as I ran that I would be right back. The police showed up to investigate the accident and said they could not do so as I was a member of the department. I was the Chaplain for the police department. They conferred and decided to call the state police. When they arrived the officer said that I was a member of their department at one time. I had started their Chaplain program.

I said at last "I am guilty someone just give me the ticket," so the State police obliged and I paid the fine. The man who hit me said he never had a problem getting a ticket.

1 Peter 2:13-14
Submit yourselves for the Lord's sake to every human authority: whether to the emperor, as the supreme authority, or to governors, who are sent by him to punish those who do wrong and to commend those who do right.

Dan Says:
"Responsibility is accepting the punishment for doing wrong as well as doing what is right."

# Moments of Ministry

# June 15

How can you be angry, embarrassed and full of joy at the same time? Have your dad come with you to get a marriage license. The stupid rule said a man had to be twenty-one years of age, but women only eighteen. Here I was nineteen and madly in love and what should have been a great experience was not turning out that way. My father the whole time was trying to talk Maxine out of marrying me. When we got to the city hall I realized I did not have enough money and had to borrow five dollars from my dad. Even though this was one of the worst days in my life it led to the very best. I got to marry the girl of my dreams and we still are together despite all the people that thought we would never last. That was in nineteen fifty-seven and here we are still together and more in love now than we were then.

Matthew 19:5
'For this reason a man will leave his father and mother and be united to his wife, and the two will become one flesh'

Dan Says:
"Love really does conquer all, no matter how you start, stay the course and enjoy the life."

# Moments of Ministry

# June 16

This was going to be wonderful; my children were not going to be raised in the city. We had bought a house in the suburbs with the assistance of Maxine's mom who lent us the down payment for a house. So here I was a city boy with a house that had walls that did not touch the house next door. I felt like a land baron with all this property. I was in the hardware store buying supplies for the yard when I spotted a chainsaw, now that's a man's tool. I bought it and started to trim in the yard, it was just great. Soon my wife came out of the house and said if I did not shut off the saw we would have no shrubbery at all. I guess I did get carried away. But it all grew back and we did have a nice yard in spite of what I had done.

Proverbs 8:19
My fruit is better than fine gold; what I yield surpasses choice silver.

Dan Says:
"Every new tool requires a learning curve, especially the Bible."

# Moments of Ministry

# June 17

Many men are blessed with wonderful children and I am pleased to say that I am one of those men. However, I am doubly blessed as both of my daughter's married wonderful husbands, strong Christian men that love the Lord and live their lives accordingly. One of my sons in law still works, but always has time to come to my aid when I need him. I am looking forward to the day he retires so he can join me and my other son in law as we fish, play golf and attend Bible studies together. My family spends vacations together and we make sure to have a family meal at least once a week. I sometimes feel that I must be a favorite of The Lord because of the way he blesses me. I have found that if you put Jesus in the center of your family and pray for them daily that God does listen and answers. It always helps to have married a woman who daily spends much time praying for all of us.

1 Timothy 3:4
He must manage his own family well and see that his children obey him, and he must do so in a manner worthy of full respect.

Dan Says:
"Happy wife...happy house."

# Moments
## of Ministry

# June 18

When you come on the dog unit of the police department the first thing you must do is find a dog. We have many people who want to donate a dog for various reasons and we test the dog to see if they will be able to do the work required. The first thing we test for is whether the dog is brave. We attempt to make him back down and if he does we cannot use him. I finally got my dog after many dogs were tested and the training began in earnest. The handler as well as the dog must be trained and the process is long and involved. The hardest thing to teach a dog is to bite on command. The dog is also trained in obedience by walking several times a day. Once while walking my dog at a super market he walked by a woman and bit her on the leg. I had a very difficult time explaining to the woman why I was praising the dog for the bite. Luckily the woman saw the badge on the dog and as it did not draw blood she forgave us and said she understood what had happened.

Psalm 143:10
Teach me to do your will, for you are my God; may your good Spirit lead me on level ground.

Dan Says:
"Yes you can teach old dog new tricks, but you must have patience."

# Moments
## of Ministry

# June 19

My mother loved to cook and she would always cook enough for unexpected guests should they arrive unexpectedly. I never had to worry about inviting someone to dinner because I knew we would always have enough food. Even in the hard times during the war there was always enough food for all to eat. There was one requirement however whatever food you put on your plate you must eat. I can remember sitting at the table and being served liver. I just could not make myself eat it as the taste to me was terrible. I told my father I could not eat the liver so he said alright you can leave the table. The next morning when the eggs were served to everyone my plate had that same piece of liver; it was the same at lunch and even dinner. The rest of the family began to sneak me food and I was not starving. Finally my dad gave up and threw away the liver, but I had to endure the lecture about the starving kids in China. I always thought why not send them the liver and let us eat the good food.

Ephesians 6:4
Fathers, do not exasperate your children; instead, bring them up in the training and instruction of the Lord.

Dan Says:
"The best of fighters only pick the fights they can win."

# Moments of Ministry

# June 20

It was really different to have a man that really enjoyed dancing. My mother had sent me to dance lessons as a young boy at Dance Master of America. I did not like it at the time, but as I grew older I found I had a big advantage at school dances. The girls would even ask me to dance. My wife and I even won a Charleston contest at the policeman's ball. She wore a black shimmy dress and I wore knickers. Boy did the troops razz me. I did realize however that to dance was important so I taught my girls how to dance. It was a highlight of my life. And if we go some place where there is dancing we still dance together. I know I sound like an old "fuddy-duddy" but holding a beautiful woman in your arms no matter if it is your wife, daughter or granddaughter and swaying to good music is a feeling like non other.

Psalm 149:3
Let them praise his name with dancing and make music to him with timbrel and harp.

Dan Says:
"Moments of shared love with the women in your family last forever."

# Moments of Ministry

# June 21

It is Jan.1, 2014 and I have just come from the gym. You may think that I went to work out and start the New Year trying to get in better shape. That is not the case at all I went to take pictures of my wife and daughters playing basketball. The thing that I think makes this different is that my wife is seventy five years old and my daughters are in their mid fifties. They play an interesting game where each has their own ball and what I thought was chaos was really a game that they played. My wife is always a source of amazement to me she is willing to try anything. I think that her attitude about life not only keeps her young but also me as I try to keep up with her. They say you are only as old as you feel, well my wife is a teenager some of the time. I thank God that He sent her to me.

Proverbs 18:22
He who finds a wife finds what is good and receives favor from the Lord.

Dan Says:
"Real joy comes from living with someone who refuses to grow old."

# MOMENTS OF MINISTRY

# June 22

As I came around the turn I could feel the back wheel losing its grip on the pavement. It finally broke loose and the bike started down on its side. I was watching the crash bar giving off all kinds of sparks and could actually see it disintegrate as I contained the slide on my side. The motorist that I was chasing did not stop; in fact he gave me a one-finger salute as he drove off. The bike stopped and I was able to crawl out from under it and use the radio to get help and put out a description of the suspect vehicle. As other officers came on the scene one of them said, "Check your revolver". I looked down at it and the walnut wood on the handle was ground away. Glad the bike went down on this side and not the other, or that would have been my hip. It took a couple of weeks but I finally found that driver and he got a healthy ticket along with a vehicle inspection to receive even more citations.

Psalm 46:1
God is our refuge and strength, an ever-present help in trouble.

Dan Says:
"You can run but you cannot hide forever."

# Moments
## of Ministry

# June 23

As I walked toward the surgeon he told me to go get a hip x-ray before I came into his office. I thought he was crazy as it was my knee that was hurting me. I complied with his request and soon I was seated in his office. He showed me the x-ray and sure enough it was a bad hip. He replaced the hip and the knee stopped hurting it was amazing. I asked him what had happened as it made no sense to me. He explained that when one part of the body is out of whack it can cause problems in other parts of the body. As a pastor it made sense to me because that is exactly what happens in the church. I now look over every situation very carefully before I decide what the real problem might be. It has saved me a lot of trouble and caused me to carefully consider decisions that can affect the Lord's church.

Job 34:24
Without inquiry he shatters the mighty and sets up others in their place.

Dan Says:
"Take time to check then double check and when you are sure check once more."

# Moments
## of Ministry

# June 24

One of the things that I did before every time I went out on duty was to shine my shoes, brass and silver star, but mostly my silver star. You see, I learned in the service that you could show pride in your work by your appearance. If you looked squared away, you acted like you were. I have worked with sloppy cops and the work they did showed they had no pride in their profession. If you wanted to you could be sloppy until an inspection and then get everything squared away, but you fooled no one. Having pride in what you are should show in everything you do and how you treat yourself and others. I treated the dirtiest drunk just like he was chief of police, and it paid off I did not have half of the fights others did. Every man deserves his dignity in every circumstance.

Romans 14:13
Therefore let us stop passing judgment on one another. Instead, make up your mind not to put any stumbling block or obstacle in the way of a brother or sister.

Dan Says:
"Treat others like you want to be treated."

# MOMENTS OF MINISTRY

# June 25

There was Sam, my elderly friend laying in the river and the worst part was the waders he borrowed were full of water as he fell with the opening pointed upriver. We helped him up and got the waders off of him and sat him in the sun to dry off. He said that fly-fishing is not all it is cracked up to be. I decided that maybe we had better start for home, as I did not want Sam to catch a cold. When we got home he was relating the story to his wife and explained how he fell in the river. But then he added something that really made me think. He said, "The worst part was not being able to get up, and that I had laughed at him". I apologized and asked for his forgiveness and Sam being a great man of God said sure I was forgiven. It was a real lesson on how God works no matter how we sin He just forgives.

Luke 6:37
Do not judge, and you will not be judged. Do not condemn, and you will not be condemned. Forgive, and you will be forgiven.

Dan Says:
"Never take away a man's pride."

# MOMENTS OF MINISTRY

# June 26

I had been working undercover in the Haight Asbury district in San Francisco disguised as a hippy. As part of my disguise I wore patchouli oil, which was used to cover the odor of marijuana (and I suppose body odor, too.) The work was fun and I enjoyed the whole scene with the underground movement. There were times however when I could come home for a few days. A real problem developed when I attempted to come home. My German Shepherd, Valiant would not let me in the house or get close enough to make him realize that is was indeed me. He could not get my smell because of the oil I was wearing and being dressed as a hippy and the long hair and beard. My children finally came home from school and let me in. I guess I could not blame the dog as I did not present the real me to him. I think that I still do not let the real me shine through the veneer of Christianity.

Ephesians 4:25
Therefore each of you must put off falsehood and speak truthfully to your neighbor, for we are all members of one body.

Dan Says:
"Show yourself to be who you really are, not who you want people to think you are."

# Moments of Ministry

# June 27

We arrived at the bank too late, as there were already plenty of police and unmarked vehicles there. I said to my partner "let's get a cup of coffee and something to eat." We went into the café that was next to the bank and sat down. While ordering the waitress kept moving her head to the side. She looked perplexed and made the head movement again. I finally asked her what she was doing and she told me that the man sitting at the end of the counter came in a while ago and went to the bathroom. I said that was not against the law. She then related that he had changed clothes while in the bathroom. We went over to him and when he saw us he just surrendered. Yes, it was the robber. We went next door to the bank, knocked and the manager opened the door, he had an FBI agent with him. The agent said we do not need your help as we have it covered. OK I said but I have the robber and the money. The agent said hand him over, I laughed and said you can get him at city prison.

Job 28:11
They search the sources of the rivers and bring hidden things to light.

Dan Says:
"The best place to hide is in plain sight."

# MOMENTS
## OF MINISTRY

# June 28

Our church was going well we were growing at a fast pace and no one seemed to know why. The one thing about the church was it was a man's church the senior pastor was an All-American wrestler and all the rest of the staff was hunters, fishermen or some type of athlete. My wife was put in charge of the marriage ceremony ministry; it was a difficult job working with couples that wanted to use our church to get married. She did a great job however. While I was in charge of men's ministry we had decided that we would have a bear-baiting seminar. So we had the expert hunters come with their stinky baits to show others how to bait bear. What I did not know was that my wife had arranged for a wedding that afternoon. She came into the sanctuary and was not too thrilled with the odors we had left behind. Wow we used many cans of odor spray to mask the smell, and finally get it almost usable.

John 2:2
and Jesus and his disciples had also been invited to the wedding.

Dan Says:
"Look past what you are planning to what others are also planning."

# Moments
## of Ministry

# June 29

We go to Hawaii every year and spend time as a family. There are some really nice activities that I enjoy in Kona; playing golf, swimming and sitting in the hot tub. The nicest thing of all is the lanai: an area like a porch that is outside the back door of the condo. It is the most peaceful place that I know, you can sit and read or eat your meals. It is also a wonderful place to just read or relax. It just seems like God made this little bit of heaven just for us. I can see the Pacific Ocean and the palm trees and my mind always wanders to think what a marvelous God we have that could even conceive of a place like this. I do not think that I could live there though as the pace of life is just too slow for me. I need to be busy doing something for His kingdom. But it is sure nice to get this break every year with my loved ones.

Revelation 14:13
Then I heard a voice from heaven say, "Write this: Blessed are the dead who die in the Lord from now on." "Yes," says the Spirit, "they will rest from their labor, for their deeds will follow them."

Dan Says:
"Learn to enjoy the rest that you have been given."

# Moments
## of Ministry

# June 30

During high school I was on the soccer team. One day while practicing a football came over from the side and landed in our field. I picked it up and kicked it back to the football players. The next thing I knew the football coach had come and talked to the soccer coach and suddenly I was called to go over to the football field. The coach asked me to punt the ball to the football players and I did. Next I was asked to kick some field goals and I also complied with his request. The next thing I knew I was on both the football and soccer teams at the same time. It was exciting and I did not mind playing both. However, I got bored at football and told the coach I was going to quit, as it was too much just sitting around. I guess he thought he would show me a lesson and said all right I could play line backer. He said all I had to do was to hit people. It turned out I got to play the rest of the season at that position.

1 Thessalonians 4:1
Now we ask you and urge you in the Lord Jesus to do this more and more.

Dan Says:
"You do not know what you are capable of doing until you try."


# MOMENTS OF MINISTRY

# July 1

I had a young man in my Sunday School Class who had a very difficult home life. One day I heard that he was skipping school and running with the wrong crowd. I put out the word that I wanted to talk to him and eventually he showed up at my house. As he sat in my office and related how his home life was I was shocked. Here he was red hair down to his shoulders and a big green stripe in the middle and he topped it off with a feather earring. I talked it over with my wife and we decided that I would go talk to his mother and get her permission to have him come live with us. To say it was hard would be an under statement, but after a few months the hair got cut, the earring came out and his grades went from failing to honor role. I am proud to say that the young man is married, a father and a schoolteacher. When we heard that he had a younger brother we went and got him also. All the credit belongs to the Lord as He did perform a miracle.

Matthew 9:36
When he saw the crowds, he had compassion on them, because they were harassed and helpless, like sheep without a shepherd.

Dan Says:
Look for the opportunity to share His love.

# MOMENTS OF MINISTRY

# July 2

Here it came as we stood on the corner in London an icon of the city a double-decker bus. It was bright red and my daughter was insistent that we sit on the top deck. I sat with my wife in the front seat and we had a wonderful view of all the streets and sights. But there was one problem, the front of the upper deck protruded over the driver's compartment. I was absolutely sure that we had run over a whole bunch of people at one stop. Also driving on the wrong side of the road was very disturbing especially when we went around a corner. Once my fears were gone I was able to really enjoy the freedom of sightseeing from this advantage point and we found it to be the very best way to see the sights of the city. Funny how fear turns to enjoyment when you know how everything works.

Isaiah 41:10
So do not fear, for I am with you; do not be dismayed, for I am your God.

Dan Says:
Learning is being observant of others that you want to be like.

# Moments
## of Ministry

# July 3

We had just landed at the airport in Cairo, Egypt and as we were exiting the airport we were forced to go through crowds of people. There was just a small lane that led between hundreds of people. I told my wife to hang on to her purse and I was very careful of my wallet. I still do not understand why there were so many people who came to the airport and just stood around. Soon we were placed on a bus with a guide who was explaining everything as we went to our hotel. The guide was from Cuba and was extolling the virtues of communism. I began to realize a little trick that the guide would use when she did not want you to see something. She would say look to the left and say some insane thing, soon I learned to look the other way and saw the extreme poverty of the city. As we passed the Nile we saw dead cows in the river and a few yards down a woman washing dishes in the river. I determined not to drink any water in Egypt after realizing where their water came from.

Acts 13:10
You are a child of the devil and an enemy of everything that is right! You are full of all kinds of deceit and trickery.

Dan Says:
There are those who would pervert all that is right in the name of politics.

# Moments
## of Ministry

# July 4

When he came in the door I fell in love with him. He was a beautiful boxer and he looked perfect. The man who was showing him to us was with Boxer rescue an organization that cared for dogs that were abused or abandoned. We took him home and after some thought we decided to name him John L Sullivan. Mr. Sullivan was the heavyweight champion of the world when there were bare fisted fighters. He was also the first champion to wear boxing gloves. John was a little fearful but gradually came to love and protect us. There is one flaw however he is afraid of loud noises like fireworks. So I spent the whole Fourth of July with an eighty pound dog in my lap. John still does not like loud noises but he makes up for this deficiency in the amount of love he shows us daily.

Proverbs 3:3
Let love and faithfulness never leave you; bind them around your neck, write them on the tablet of your heart.

Dan Says:
The love and faithfulness of a dog should remind us to be the same with God.

# MOMENTS OF MINISTRY

# July 5

In the class were a whole lot of people who hated me. The teacher Angelia Davis was a very radical instructor who had great sympathy for any cause that was anti-government. The school was San Francisco State College and had a long-standing riot going. We had been assigned to the college and we knew there would be a demonstration every day at noon. As long as we were there several of the men in the squad decided to take some classes. It worked out great, as the school did not charge us for the credits. I had decided that I would take the class from Ms. Davis so I could harass her. She hated me and called me a pig every day and I called her some choice names also. I think I knew how Daniel felt in the lion's den. Even though she attempted to flunk me, somehow I always ended up with a very high grade.

James 1:9
Believers in humble circumstances ought to take pride in their high position.

Dan Says:
Keep your pride in all circumstances and remember to whom you belong.

# Moments of Ministry

## July 6

As I looked over at my Grandson Josh trying to use my candlestick rotary dial phone I could not keep from laughing. He held the earpiece in one ear and the mouthpiece in the other ear. He had never seen a phone that did not have push button numbers before. It started me thinking how things have changed in my life; just in telephones when I was young we had five families on one party line and could listen in to their calls any time we wanted. Then we had our own line and felt like millionaires, next the phone in the suitcase that would sometimes work. When that brick came out I always had my wife carry it in her purse, as it was huge. Now we carry computers in our pocket that have as much power as the computers that went to the moon. We really can communicate any time or place now. You know we could always do that with God no technology needed at all.

Romans 10:13
"Everyone who calls on the name of the Lord will be saved."

Dan Says:
The most important communication is the easiest of all. He waits to hear from you.

# MOMENTS OF MINISTRY

# July 7

When we came over the hill it took my breath away. There it was Jerusalem the holy city of God. The old walls were still intact and the gates were visible, the only wrong thing was the golden dome standing where the temple should be. As I looked I could see the Golden Gate bricked up by Suleiman in the seventh century to keep the Messiah from entering. All along the mount were the ossuaries of the dead who wanted to be where the Messiah would come so they would be the first raised. How could a people who were so loved by God get it so mixed up? I knew how Jesus must have felt when he lamented "Jerusalem O Jerusalem how I wanted to gather you like a hen does her chicks under her wings". When we are told to pray for the peace of Jerusalem it is very easy when you see and feel the presence of God in this Holy Place. It is a place every Christian should experience.

John 10:1-2
Very truly I tell you Pharisees, anyone who does not enter the sheep pen by the gate, but climbs in by some other way, is a thief and a robber. The one who enters by the gate is the shepherd of the sheep.

Dan Says:
He is the only way that you can enter there is no other way. Jesus is the Shepherd

# Moments of Ministry

# July 8

When I entered the command post my partner and I were told to get to a position where we could see into the apartment. We went to the roof of a building across the street from the suspects building. As I was getting ready my spotter said that there was something strange going on. As the entry team was coming around the corner we observed a man in the apartment preparing a Molotov cocktail. That is a jar of flammable liquid with a wick of some sort. I knew if the entry team lined up at the door he would toss the firebomb at them. I got him in my sights and fired, the bomb exploded in the room he was standing in. As the building was very old the fire spread rapidly and the suspects had to flee the premises and were taken into custody. The papers the next day printed that the police had shot incendiary bullets into the house. I wished I had such a thing but there was none.

Jeremiah 31:10
'He who scattered Israel will gather them and will watch over his flock like a shepherd.'
Dan Says:
There is always someone watching over you.

# Moments of Ministry

# July 9

Bozo was a cross-trained dog, by that I mean if you said, "Come here", he ran the other way. If you said "get out of here' he came and stayed. The only one that the dog really got along with was Mike who was an alcoholic surfer I had brought home from the mission. They both were very anti-social and hated people and both had a tendency to run away every chance they got. Well Bozo had one other bad habit that almost did him in; every time I ran the chain saw he would try to attack it. I do not need to tell you that it was not a very smart thing to do. It was a habit I could not break him from doing. Well Mike had the same problem he could not stay away from booze. Bozo did not kill himself with the chainsaw, but Mike did kill himself with drugs and alcohol. Even knowing that something is really bad for us, does not keep us from it.

Romans 15:1

We who are strong ought to bear with the failings of the weak and not to please ourselves.

Dan Says:
Try as you might; only God can change a heart.

# Moments of Ministry

## July 10

I had completed my examination by the ordination council that had been called for that purpose. It was a very difficult time of answering a ton of doctrinal questions, and many questions about the Word of God. I remember the first question that was asked, "Name five cities on the road of the patriarchs" I finished the questioning after a couple of hours and then as I was examined at a Bible College I had to decide at which church my ordination ceremony would take place. I had offers from a couple of bigger churches as well as my own home church. My wife and I prayed about where we would have it and finally it came to us. We would have the ceremony at the Union Gospel Mission where I was working. It was truly wonderful as the winos and tramps watched and knew something special was happening to their friend. It was a night I will never forget.

Acts 13:3
So after they had fasted and prayed, they placed their hands on them and sent them off.

Dan Says:
Some things are extra special because you share them with special people.

# MOMENTS
## OF MINISTRY

# July 11

Because of our interest of all things Jewish, my wife and I have led many Seder dinners both in our home and in church settings. I am always amazed when we do a dinner that the participants get the true meaning of our communion. When you think of the Haggadah [ORDER OF SERVICE], the order of Jesus life had been in effect for hundreds if not thousands of years. In order to preserve the religious ceremonies of the Jewish faith not a word was changed. Then Jesus took the fourth cup the cup of praise and changed the wording and meaning of the cup. He established for us the tradition of the communion service. It was so important to Him that when He taught Paul in the book of Corinthians where he added even more to the instructions. He said that a person should examine himself to see if he is fit to take communion. What a joy to be able to remember His sacrifice after all these years.

1 Corinthians 11:23-24
For I received from the Lord what I also passed on to you: The Lord Jesus, on the night he was betrayed, took bread, and when he had given thanks, he broke it and said, "This is my body, which is for you; do this in remembrance of me."

Dan Says:
We cry about ten percent; He gave it all.

# MOMENTS
## OF MINISTRY

## July 12

We lived on Potrero Hill in San Francisco. It was an older ethnic neighborhood that was mostly old Italians and Russians. The people were nice to be around and would drop whatever they were doing to help a neighbor. One the corner was a very old Italian man who would make his own wine. One day I noticed that he got a delivery of grapes and was struggling to get them to his vat in the basement. I jumped in and gave him a hand and we got all of the grapes to the basement. Some months later the old man came to our apartment and gave us a few bottles of wine and he said for me a special bottle of Grappa. We soon found that the Grappa was home made liquor that made Irish whiskey seem mild. The old man told me how he was very popular during prohibition and that he made the best booze in town.

Ecclesiastes 4:9
Two are better than one, because they have a good return for their labor:

Dan Says:
Real love is shown by real work helping others in time of need.

# Moments of Ministry

# July 13

I came into the station and was told to go to the chief's office right away. I was wondering what trouble I was in now as I headed down the hall. I noticed that as I passed each office the people inside would come out of their office to follow me. So the whole parade came to the Chief's office and there were way too many to get into his office so we all went to dispatch where there was enough room for all. With a great flourish the chief presented to me a new cell phone, this one was different that most as it was adorned with several balloons. The chief said maybe this would help it to float. I had lost my two previous phones, one in the river and the other in the lake. You know you are making progress with the department when they feel they can make fun of you.

Luke 19:10
For the Son of Man came to seek and to save the lost.

Dan Says:
Live your life so everyone can enjoy it.

# Moments of Ministry

## July 14

As I was walking down the street people were giving me strange looks. I was on the way to my father's workplace to show him my new teeth. I was only fourteen years old when I developed a bad gum disease that caused my teeth to be extremely soft and break very easily. My family did not have a lot of money so my parents decided to have all of my teeth pulled and dentures placed in my mouth. I came from Painless Parkers office to show my dad first. When he saw me he was shocked and brought me to the bathroom where there was a mirror. I was bleeding all over the front of me, I did not realize because of the painkiller that was administered. Now this might sound bad to some, but it was a wonderful thing for me to have straight white teeth and the ability to be able to bite and chew anything. Actually my new appearance gave me a new confidence to live my life.

1 Samuel 16:7
"Do not consider his appearance or his height, for I have rejected him. The Lord does not look at the things people look at. People look at the outward appearance, but the Lord looks at the heart."

Dan Says:
God did not make us all beautiful, but we should do our best with what he gave us.

# Moments of Ministry

## July 15

We rented a bus and the whole Dog Pack (our senior group at church) was on our way to the Seattle, Washington area where the beautiful tulip fields were located. We were singing and joking and generally having a good time. Soon we entered the area of the field and imagine our surprise when all we saw were stems sticking out of the ground. We had arrived a few days after the harvest. We decided to go see the tulips anyway the only difference was we would see them is bundles at the Farmers Market in Seattle. After we had toured the market and had wonderful seafood we went to spend the night in Leavenworth, Washington and had a nice time of eating and touring before we came home. The flexibility of this group was a wonderful thing to behold. They could enjoy anything as long as we did it together.

1 John 1:6
If we claim to have fellowship with him and yet walk in the darkness, we lie and do not live out the truth.

Dan Says:
Love prevails when Jesus is present.

# Moments
## of Ministry

## July 16

My granddaughter who was traveling through England with family had only one thought in mind, a plain cheese sandwich with pickles. After dinner one night she ordered pudding and did not realize that some pudding in London was made from blood and was not pleasant to American taste. We had all been very careful when ordering food in England. Amy ordered a cheese sandwich with pickles and when we got on the train she opened the wrapper and said, "Guess what color my pickle is?" She had gotten a pickled turnip and it was brown. She finally got to a restaurant and saw an egg sandwich on the menu. She questioned the waitress as to ingredients in the sandwich. She asked if it was plain bread, egg and mayonnaise, and nothing else. The waitress assured her by telling her that's all that was in the sandwich. After some more thought Amy asked "Is that egg from a chicken?" The waitress gave a laugh and said, "Of course."

1 Corinthians 3:18
Do not deceive yourselves. If any of you think you are wise by the standards of this age, you should become "fools" so that you may become wise.

Dan Says:
Always check the desires of your heart, make sure they line up with God's desires for you.

# Moments
## of Ministry

# July 17

Late in life I discovered gardening and I find great solace in my vegetable garden. I set off a piece of land and turn it over and add ingredients that I am sure you would not want on your table. The dog enjoyed them however and loved to roll in them. I then fenced in a portion of the yard to keep my dog out. Not being a farmer I planted a lot of things that would not grow in this climate. Other plants took special care I knew nothing about so they did not grow. I think some grew by accident and would grow anywhere. The next year I did research and was very selective in what I planted and did a little better. I finally got the secret in my third year of planting, I prayed over every plant and seed. If one would not grow I would say it was of the Devil and pull it up. That prayed for produce was really tasty and if I forgot grace, it was prayed for anyway.

Genesis 3:17
Cursed is the ground because of you; through painful toil you will eat food from it all the days of your life.

Dan Says:
While you are on your knees plucking out weeds, you might as well pray.

# Moments
## of Ministry

# July 18

I had come in off the beat at four in the morning so I could do some checking in the records department in the Hall of Justice. As I got off of the elevator I heard a shot and a lot of commotion I drew my pistol and very carefully exited the elevator car and crept forward to the hallway where the shots came from. As soon as I turned the corner I saw a man running with several men chasing him. I took my shooters stance feet wide apart, both hands on the gun and got him in my sights. As he turned around and saw me he screamed like a little girl and fell to the floor. I then noticed how bright it was in the hall and soon saw what was happening. They were filming a movie in the building. It turned out for good as from then on they hired off duty cops to guard them.

Psalm 140:1
Rescue me, Lord, from evildoers; protect me from the violent,

Dan Says:
Be cautious when you feel fear, but remember He protects.

# Moments
## of Ministry

# July 19

He had a full house and was sure he was going to win the hand. We were at work playing a friendly game of poker. This particular hand was getting out of control fast. Up to this point I had been winning and one of the guys was getting upset. When he couldn't take it any longer, he said, "I bet you my car against the money you have in front of you." I agreed and that is how I got my Goggomobil. It was a car made by Bavarian Motor Works in Germany. It is a very small car. It only held four gallons of gas and got eighty miles to the gallon. I wish I had it now. The wheels were so small that once I hit a big puddle in the road and the car floated. The Goggomobil was light enough that the neighborhood kids had much delight in relocating the car onto my porch. It was a fun car while it lasted and definitely a great conversation piece.

Proverbs 19:19
A hot-tempered person must pay the penalty; rescue them, and you will have to do it again.

Dan Says:
Never bet against a man with four sixes.

# Moments
## of Ministry

# July 20

When you are in the police academy you have to wear khaki pants and a light blue shirt. For weeks and weeks all you think about is one day I will wear a real police uniform. I will not be recognized as a rookie anymore but an actual police officer. The day finally arrived and I was going to graduate from the Academy. I was as shiny as I could be, spit shined my leather and that badge was shining brighter than the stars it represented. My name was called and I received my first salute as a patrolman. I was never more proud than in that moment. As time went on my uniform was not as neat as it was at first. The shoes were not as shiny, neither was my badge. I had gotten used to putting on that uniform every day and the thrill was gone. Sounds a lot like when I accepted The Lord. I was as proud as I could be and all knew where I stood. However, as time went by, I became less and less as excited as I was at first. Later on down the road I found that old star. I polished it up and it is just as beautiful as before. I don't think it is too late to get my walk with the Lord back to what it was before.

Revelation 22:14
Blessed are those who wash their robes, that they may have the right to the tree of life and may go through the gates into the city.

Dan Says:
God gets us clean, but we have to keep on cleaning ourselves.

# MOMENTS OF MINISTRY

# July 21

We have a concept at our church where everything is team oriented. I sometimes have a problem with people who want to be on a team, but have no point of reference. When you are on a team you have to put aside what you want and find out what is best for the team. When I first started playing sand lot football as a child, we found out that everybody wanted to be quarterback. No one said, "I will center the ball." All of us wanted to be the star. When the coach gave us the concept of "team", he would look us over and decide who would be best for the whole group. As I went on through the years I became involved with other teams. As a police officer I was on a tactical team that was often placed in life threatening situations. That team was certainly different from a team of people working at a church. But the concepts will always remains the same, love and protect those you depend on as they depend on you.

Proverbs 28:26
Those who trust in themselves are fools, but those who walk in wisdom are kept safe.

Dan Says:
If it is about you, it is not team.

# MOMENTS
## OF MINISTRY

# July 22

I was on my four-day weekend when I got the call. I was told not to shave and to report to the Presidio Military Hospital on Tuesday morning. I there was met by a military policeman and taken to a room where they placed a hammerless thirty-eight in my hand and then placed a cast on it. I was told to go home and wait for further instructions. After two more days (my wife would not sleep with me), I got the call to report to the detective bureau. Where I met my partner who was dressed as a gay man in girls clothing... I laughed and said I got the best of this deal, I was to be a wino and very dirty and my partner was a cross dresser who had a very large purse. He had a sawed off shotgun in his purse. We found that there were some people who were intending to free some prisoners from a courtroom. We had their photos and took them by surprise as they entered the court.

> Matthew 24:4
> Jesus answered: "Watch out that no one deceives you."

> Dan Says:
> What you see is not always what you get.

# MOMENTS OF MINISTRY

# July 23

We were all on a diet, the whole family and working hard at losing weight. When we could not stand it any longer we would go out to eat just so we could have something different. There was always the pact to be made that we would support each other in keeping with our diets. After studying the menu and having discussion about what was the healthiest food on the menu we all decided that chicken was the best choice. I watched my wife order her chicken broiled, my two daughters gave it much thought and then went along with their mother and ordered their chicken prepared the same way. The waitress looked at me and said, "What can I do for you?" I replied, "I will have chicken fried steak." My family called me a cheater, but I enjoyed every bite.

Matthew 4:4
Jesus answered, "It is written: 'Man shall not live on bread alone, but on every word that comes from the mouth of God.'"

Dan Says:
Just by the use of words you can change the intention, so beware.

# Moments
## of Ministry

## July 24

Addiction is a horrible thing to have happen to you; it causes you to become something that you know in your heart you are not. It sneaks up on you and you do not even realize that it is happening. By the time you know what has happened it is too late and all your time and energy only wants to support your addiction. I saw myself as I really was and it was not very pretty. I began to have problems at work, but the real problems were at home. I was hurting my family constantly by lying and even spending money that should have gone into the household. Finally, I reached a point that I even hated myself I was a total wreck. When I turned myself in to my boss he just smiled and said, "We will get you help." I was sent to a detox center in the country and there I was introduced to AA (Alcoholics Anonymous). I saw what good it would do and attended several meeting, but in my heart I was already planning my next drunk. Totally disgusted with myself I went to my room and cried out" God I do not believe you are there, but if you are take control of my life as it is impossible for me". He did not answer audibly but I have never taken a drink from that day until now. What a GREAT GOD.

Romans 8:35
Who shall separate us from the love of Christ? Shall trouble or hardship or persecution or famine or nakedness or danger or sword?

Dan Says:
When you cannot, He can.

# MOMENTS OF MINISTRY

# July 25

When we moved to Post Falls, Idaho, it was a small town and it even had a general store. The store sat on a corner of the main street. This store had everything you could possibly want to purchase. The trouble was you had to search to find anything, but nonetheless, it was still a fun store to shop at. The most amazing thing about this store was the roof. The roof was full of life-sized animals of every kind. There was one animal in particular that was of interest to me, a life sized pig. Now being a retired cop I thought that a pig in the yard would be great. I went into the store and talked to the owner and asked if I could purchase the pig. She was indignant and said under no circumstances would she sell the pig. I sheepishly left the store. The very next day the pig was stolen and I was sure that she thought I did it. As luck would have it the pig was recovered, some high school kids did it as a prank. It was nice to be off the hook.

Proverbs 3:30
Do not accuse anyone for no reason—when they have done you no harm.

Dan Says:
Watch that your desires do not entrap you.

# MOMENTS
## OF MINISTRY

# July 26

You would think it would be easier after all these years to find the right present for my wife's birthday. We got married when she was eighteen, now what is the right gift for a beautiful seventy five year old wife. I have over the years tried clothes and for some reason she does not think much of my taste. I have given her jewelry and she wears it for a while and then it goes into the jewel box. A trip would be fine, but we have some in the works already. Then it came like a flash I went to the Sports Authority store at the mall and bought her a wonderful Pink Basketball. The clerk when I purchased the ball said my granddaughter would love it. She was quite surprised when I said it was for my wife. I then explained how my wife and two daughters who are in their fifties enjoy playing basketball together.

Proverbs 17:6
Children's children are a crown to the aged, and parents are the pride of their children.

Dan Says:
Youth is truly wasted on the young.

# Moments of Ministry

# July 27

After a lifetime of watching movies about London when we went there we had a list of must do things. One was to eat in a pub or what we would call a bar. We had been told the best food was in pubs, so off we went to find a pub for dinner. We sat and looked at a menu that made absolutely no sense to any of us. I have learned over the years when in doubt order breakfast. So I asked for an English breakfast the waitress asked if I wanted bangers or rashers with my eggs I took a chance and said bangers. It turned out to be a good choice as bangers turned out to be sausage. My wife ordered a luncheon type of meal and when she decided that she would like soup also she could not get the waitress to respond to her gestures or even when she called. She finally went up to her and asked for soup with her meal. The waitress so 'no you already ordered". We were all surprised by the remark, but that was the way in London Pubs.

1 John 2:17
The world and its desires pass away, but whoever does the will of God lives forever.

Dan Says:
We do not always get what we want, that might be best for us.

# Moments
## of Ministry

# July 28

I was walking the beat on Sixth Street during the mid watch and it was quiet. I was enjoying myself talking to all my regulars, the newspaper vendor the merchants who always loved it when you entered their place of business. The weather was really nice and I was in a shirt and no jacket and enjoying a beautiful afternoon. Then suddenly a man rushed up to me and said there was a big fight at the Hot Spot Tavern. When I entered the premises I could see several people involved in an altercation. What I always attempted to do in these situations was to find the biggest participant and smack him either with my Club or my lead lined gloves. I spotted a large Samoan and hit him as hard as I could. He turned and smiled at me and then proceeded to knock me under a pinball machine. Every time I tried to get out from under he would push me back under. I finally said, "If you let me out I will buy you a beer". He let me out and I went to get help. When we tried to handcuff the man the cuffs would not fit. I ended up giving him a note and told him to turn himself in at the station. To my surprise he did just that, when I came in to make a report there he was. I let him go with a warning and from then on he would protect me when he could.

Hebrews 1:14
Are not all angels ministering spirits sent to serve those who will inherit salvation?

Dan Says:
Angels come in all sizes and shapes.

# Moments of Ministry

# July 29

My wife decided that I needed to spend more time with my kids, so she volunteered for me to go to a campout with my daughter's sixth grade class. Now you have to realize that these teachers were as liberal as they could possibly get. They spent a lot of time drinking wine and saying how bad the system was. I lasted through the whole weekend without hitting or even cussing out these people. The time came for us to go home and I was so happy I could cry. Coming down the highway we spotted a wreck, a car had gone into a canal off the road. I jumped into the water and brought the driver up to the road. He was in bad shape and I could see he was heading into shock. I asked him if he was diabetic and he replied that he was. I called for a candy bar into a bus of sixth graders and soon had many to choose from. The man ate the bar and immediately became better. The kids were amazed at what happened, but mostly my daughter was as proud as she could be. What could have been a disaster in more than one way turned out to be wonderful for a sixth grade girl.

Psalm 37:3
Trust in the Lord and do good; dwell in the land and enjoy safe pasture.

Dan Says:
Never give up trying to do good.

# Moments of Ministry

# July 30

During World War 2 this nation came to the front, as everyone was involved in the war effort. I can remember that sacrifice was thought of as being natural. There was a concerted attempt to see that those who were fighting got everything they needed to accomplish the task of defeating the enemy. One way was to grow your own vegetables. So any plot of dirt in the city was converted to growing produce and the war effort was enhanced because of the willingness of people to do their part. These little plots of ground had a name given to them that tells the whole story they were called Victory Gardens. Every little old man and woman did their part to win the war, and they were successful. With everyone doing their part the enemy was defeated. What if we had this attitude in our war with the forces of evil? We have the ability to win; we just have to get it done.

Proverbs 14:23
All hard work brings a profit, but mere talk leads only to poverty.

Dan Says:
If we all come together we will be victors.

# Moments
## of Ministry

# July 31

We were sitting outside on a balcony in Hawaii having breakfast and looking at the Pacific Ocean. There were wonderful fruit bearing trees and the weather was fabulous and warm. We had just come from the snowstorms of Idaho and this was like heaven to us. We ordered breakfast and had the tasty Kona coffee as well as exotic fruit juice to start the meal... Then another party of people was seated near us. Everything went downhill fast as this group had a loud mouth in it. He spoke so everyone in the restaurant could hear all he had to say. Every word that proceeded from his mouth was a bald faced lie. He spoke of swimming with sharks and petting them and then the stories became even more bizarre. The whole atmosphere changed and all we wanted to do was to get away from this nut. It's strange how a perfect stranger can affect your whole day. I hope I can change someone's day also, but for good as I speak of The Lord.

2 Timothy 2:15
Do your best to present yourself to God as one approved, a worker who does not need to be ashamed and who correctly handles the word of truth.

Dan Says:
Like the snake in the garden we had a big mouth in our paradise.

# Moments of Ministry

# August 1

We were all packed and ready to start a weeklong camping trip with the family. We stopped first at the police department picnic; I thought it would be a great way to start our vacation. The food was very good and then games were about to start. My wife begged me not to play softball as she said I would hurt my very fragile back. Naturally I did not listen and was soon playing my heart out, you guessed it I dove for a ground ball and felt my back go out. I came to the picnic table and said it was time to go on the campout. The pain was unbelievable I could hardly drive the car. My wife said, "Did you throw out your back?" I said, "Just a little." Then my daughter came up to us and said that I looked like the letter Z. I guess that there's no hiding it; at times I can be one of the world's dumbest people.

Luke 24:25
He said to them, "How foolish you are, and how slow to believe all that the prophets have spoken!

Dan Says:
Stupid is hearing, but never listening.

# Moments of Ministry

# August 2

I am downtown San Francisco at the turnstile of the cable car and back on pickpocket detail again. The head of the detail would use me on occasion when a new group of pickpockets came to town or when making too many arrests burned him out. We were on the third floor looking out a window and the boss was showing me the suspected pickers at work. It looked like we had some visiting gangs in town, as there were at least four working as we watched. One was a young Gypsy girl who was a distraction while her partner made the pick. She was about eighteen and well endowed. Her blouse was cut dangerously low barley concealing her assets. The mark or victim was so engrossed looking down her blouse that her accomplice could have removed his socks. When we did make the arrest they had over thirty credit cards of different people.

Matthew 5:29
If your right eye causes you to stumble, gouge it out and throw it away.

Dan Says:
Put a rubber band around your wallet and it will be hard to steal.

# Moments
## of Ministry

# August 3

I was chasing a speeder on my motorcycle when a car made a left hand turn in front of me. I had no time to hit the brakes or lay the bike down so I hit it broadside. The bike stopped and I did not, I flew quite a distance before landing on both arms. My partner came up to me and by the look on his face I knew it was not good news. I remember I asked him to put my arm on my chest and he said "no way". Well I had broken both arms and I want to tell you that stunk. I could not wash, shave or do any normal thing. The worst was eating. I was dependent on my family to feed me like a baby. Sometime they would forget and I would put my face in the plate and eat like a dog. Then they would say, "Dad, quit being so dramatic". It might have been the worst six weeks of my life. But because of the love and care of my family I made it through that terrible time.

Psalm 121:1
I lift up my eyes to the mountains—where does my help come from?

Dan Says:
Love and treat your family well, you may need them someday.

# MOMENTS OF MINISTRY

# August 4

The fanciest hotel that I ever stayed in was in Amman, Jordan. My wife and I were not hicks that could be amazed by our surroundings but this place was opulent. We had gone down to the lobby and there was some kind of Saudi royal with his entourage. As we stared I noticed a woman in western dress that did not seem to fit in with the whole scene. She had on a nice suit and high heel shoes. I was surprised when she turned around and had a scarf over her face so all I could see was her eyes. When we arrived at our room we had a balcony that overlooked a park. I saw and heard a great commotion going on and I looked down and saw some Bedouins putting up a tent in the park. The police had to finally arrest them and take them away. I asked a waiter about this and he said they do it every year. They say they have put their tent there for ten thousand years. Funny to see how the west meets the east in the same block.

Proverbs 29:13
The poor and the oppressor have this in common: The Lord gives sight to the eyes of both.

Dan Says:
Scratch the skin of an apple and inside they are all the same.

# Moments of Ministry

# August 5

While taking my police dog for his daily obedience walk I was passing a house with an open garage door. The woman of the house had been shopping and was unloading her car. My dog was off leash for a few moments of just walking and doing dog things. All of a sudden without warning my dog, Shelby ran into this ladies garage just as she used an automatic door opener to shut the door. I called but it was too late. I went up to the door of the house and rang the bell. No answer. I knocked on the door also no answer. I finally pounded on the door in desperation but again no answer. I yelled to the woman inside and tried to tell her she had a large dog in her garage and by now he was probably not very happy. Just then the police car appeared and the officer told me to hold up my hands. I showed him my star and explained what had happened. The woman finally came out of the house and said I could go and get my dog. She did not believe me until she saw that the dog had a badge just like mine.

Micah 7:5
Do not trust a neighbor; put no confidence in a friend.

Dan Says:
Loving your neighbor is hard to do if you do not know them.

# Moments of Ministry

# August 6

There are times in your life that just have special meaning and could never be forgotten. One of those times for me was when my granddaughter had finished her training and was ready to receive her badge as a police dispatcher. She was the one in my family who had decided to follow me in law enforcement. I was so proud I could almost bust as the Chief asked me to come up and pin Amy. She was the best dispatcher that this or any other department could ever have. Of course I might be just a little prejudiced in this assessment. But I saw her in action I was called to the dispatch one evening as several patrol cars were chasing a man who was wanted. One of the officers involved in the chase was my granddaughter's boy friend. The chase ended in a shooting and she handled the situation with great efficiency. After we heard that the suspect was down and no officers hurt she came a got a big hug. I could then just be Grandpa.

1 Peter 4:11
If anyone serves, they should do so with the strength God provides, so that in all things God may be praised through Jesus Christ.

Dan Says:
In time of great stress Jesus always come through.

# Moments of Ministry

# August 7

When you are the worst of all sinners you sometimes feel that there is absolutely no hope for you. This is the attack that the enemy uses to make you feel unworthy and unwanted. But it is a lie from the pit of hell. When I was at my worst in my addiction to alcoholism my loving family never gave up on me. When I came out of the detox center a new man in Christ my family gave me an opportunity to show I had changed. It was a most difficult time for me as I knew I had changed, but my family had heard that tune before. It was necessary for me to prove myself to my wife and children. I had to earn the right to be the man of the house all over again. When I made a decision the children would look at my wife to see if it was all right to do as I said. My wife had to let me become the head of household again. I am so grateful to God that He led her to allow me to once again gain the love and respect of my children. I now have a wonderful family who all love and follow Jesus.

Luke 6:37
Do not judge, and you will not be judged. Do not condemn, and you will not be condemned. Forgive, and you will be forgiven.

Dan Says:
Who said there are no miracles now days?

# Moments
## of Ministry

# August 8

We had just come from the archeological site in Corinth .The site was wonderful we had seen the temple to Aphrodite high up on the mountain surrounding the city. The dig was in progress and we saw the Agora {market place} and the synagogue where Paul did years worth of preaching. The most exciting place for me was the Bema {Judgment seat} where they had taken the synagogue president for a judgment about Christianity. It was at this place that the new religion was declared legal in the Roman Empire. After a wonderful lunch at a local restaurant we boarded the bus I asked what was the best thing you saw at this historical site. One man answered "the first public toilets "I knew what he said was true, but I was saddened by his lack of Biblical Knowledge. I guess that there is a difference in the way we view things.

1 Corinthians 11:2
I praise you for remembering me in everything and for holding to the traditions just as I passed them on to you.

Dan Says:
You can teach and teach, but you cannot make them learn.

# Moments
## of Ministry

# August 9

I was invited to a wedding so I went and bought a new leisure suit as they were right in style. I had to have the suit altered but did not have time to have the tailor shop do the alterations. My daughter had taken up sewing and she was very good at it. I came home with the suit and asked her if she could please alter the suit. She asked me to try it on but I was busy so I said just do it to the same size as some other pants. I went to work and when I got home I asked if she had finished my pants and she replied that she had. Well the day of the wedding I put on the pants and they were way short in the legs. I was really angry, but she reminded me she asked me to try them on. There was very little cuff to let down so I went to the wedding looking like I expected a flood at any time. Needless to say many of my friends had comments about my attire. I did however learn a valuable lesson. Stop and take the time to get it right.

Hebrews 2:1
We must pay the most careful attention, therefore, to what we have heard, so that we do not drift away.

Dan Says:
When someone wants to do you a favor, do it their way.

# MOMENTS OF MINISTRY

# August 10

My family lives on a diet we all tend to be the body type that puts on weight that shows. When I was young I tried to put on weight and no matter how I tried it would not come on me. After a few years that certainly was not a problem anymore. I passed those genes to my girls and they always have to watch their weight also. When we first moved to Idaho we decided that this was a new beginning and we should all lose weight. We were very good and stayed on our food program, but we always wanted something sweet preferably chocolate. When we could not stand it any longer my wife came up with an idea. We would save all of our calories for the day and she would make a big chocolate cake and cut it into four pieces and we would satisfy our cravings. We did and from that day on all I could think about was chocolate.

Proverbs 23:6
Do not eat the food of a begrudging host, do not crave his delicacies;

Dan Says:
You should not eat what you want to stay away from that's stupid.

# Moments
## of Ministry

# August 11

I had finished a nice Israeli breakfast and was taking a walk through the old city in Jerusalem. I was walking in the Arab quarter and was just strolling along soaking up the foreign atmosphere when I got that sudden urge that tells you that something you ate did not sit well. I knew that I had to find a rest room fast and right away. I was frantically looking about when there it was a public rest room. Now if you have never had the experience of an Arab public rest room you are very fortunate indeed. You stand on two metal feet that is in the middle of a channel that carries away waste. There are no walls or seats and the worst of all no toilet paper. I realized that I had to sacrifice my handkerchief at this time. Right after throwing the hankie away I knew I had more to do. When I finished this time I took a few dollar bills and used them to wipe. When I threw them into the channel a fight erupted to retrieve the money. I got out as fast as I could.

Proverbs 23:4
Do not wear yourself out to get rich; do not trust your own cleverness.

Dan Says:
Try and be more careful with your money!!

# MOMENTS OF MINISTRY

# August 12

When we got the opportunity to be able to move out of the city limits we were very happy and began a home search at once. We found a nice home in Mill Valley across the Golden Gate Bridge. This town is located in Marin County the most liberal county in the west at this time. I tried to get along, but it was difficult for me. I finally found some friends at the local bowling alley. One night when I showed up to bowl the whole league was advised that our cost for bowling had been paid for the entire season. One of the bowlers had struck it rich. His name was George Lucas and he had a hit movie come out named "Star Wars". It's strange how this guy went from George to Mr. Lucas in one night.

Exodus 20:7
You shall not misuse the name of the Lord your God, for the Lord will not hold anyone guiltless who misuses his name.

Dan Says:
Respect everyone, but respect God more.

# MOMENTS
## OF MINISTRY

# August 13

The building we found for the church was round and we said we can say come here and you won't get cornered. The floor plan just did not work for a house but we thought it would be fine for a small church. It would certainly be better than the garage we were meeting in. I was asked to try and get supplies for remodeling the building. I went to a local mill and asked about getting some four-inch tongue and groove cedar. The owner of the mill made me a great deal on the lumber it was so good I asked if I could add to the order for lumber to remodel my house. He said yes and the project started. I did several rooms and was using the last of the scraps to do some trim work. I had gotten down to the very last piece and was running it through the saw and instead of getting a pusher I use my hands on a very small piece. I heard a funny sound and then saw all the blood. Sure enough I cut off the ends of two fingers, just being stupid again.

2 Corinthians 8:11
Now finish the work, so that your eager willingness to do it may be matched by your completion of it, according to your means.

Dan Says:
Do you're very best right up to the very end.

# Moments
## of Ministry

# August 14

I was on leave from the Navy and very excited to see my girlfriend. I had a huge surprise for her; I had saved up and was able to buy a diamond ring at the PX (Post Exchange). Over and over I had practiced what I was going to say to her as I asked her to be my wife. My whole family was aware that I was going to pop the question and my mother got really excited and even planned an engagement party. I was very nervous when I got to Amy's house but things got better when I found her parents were not home. I guided her to the couch and in my sweetest voice I popped the question "Will you marry me?" I was shocked when after very little thought she looked at me and said "No". I told her she had no choice as she had at least to wear the ring tonight as we had an engagement party to attend. Well she put on the ring and never took it off thank God.

Ephesians 5:33
However, each one of you also must love his wife as he loves himself, and the wife must respect her husband.

Dan Says:
Persistence in the right things pays great reward.

# Moments of Ministry

# August 15

Injured again in the line of duty not bad enough to be off work, but enough so I could not be on the street. I was assigned to the warrant bureau and it was boring to the absolute maximum. We had the warrants in large rotating bins in alphabetical order and when someone would call for a check we would search through the bin. Well we really got high tech and installed the first computer. I was working the midnight shift and everything was really quiet so I decided to take a nap on my lunch hour. The only problem was the stupid computer was always clanking away. I finally walked over and pulled the plug for a while so I could nap. The next day I heard the bosses talking about how the computer for the whole state was shut down and no one could find the reason for the crash. I kept my mouth shut and did not turn it off anymore.

James 1:19
My dear brothers and sisters, take note of this: Everyone should be quick to listen, slow to speak and slow to become angry,

Dan Says:
How easy to turn off what we do not want to hear.

# Moments of Ministry

# August 16

While visiting a friend who lives in the Seattle area with my daughter and son in law, we had the pleasure of meeting Shasta. She was a rescued greyhound that had loads of personality. We got to go to the park with her and watch her run. She was really fast and fun to observe. When we went back to the apartment where the dog and her owner lived we sat in the living room and talked. The dog came up behind me and licked my head. She then proceeded to gag. We all laughed and then she did it a second time and gagged even worse. Her owner told the dog to stop licking me before she really got sick. I guess you can see how that made me feel.

Psalm 34:8
Taste and see that the Lord is good; blessed is the one who takes refuge in him.

Dan Says:
It is all a matter of taste, but it is not always our taste that counts.

# Moments of Ministry

# August 17

One of my fondest memories when I was a child was our Sunday ritual of listening to the radio. I would lie on the floor and the programs would start coming on. Really good shows like Gang Busters, The Shadow, Life of Riley and many others. You listened and were transported in your mind to different places and times and you had to use your imagination.

I remember once when my Dad was listening to a ball game he said that someday they would be playing ball in New York and we would see it in San Francisco. I was sure that he was crazy to even think of such a thing.

Proverbs 10:14
The wise store up knowledge, but the mouth of a fool invites ruin.

Dan Says:
Do not make your life so simple that you forget to live it.

# Moments of Ministry

# August 18

There were many great soccer games that I was involved in when I was a teenager. But the most difficult game was one that I played against my brother. He was playing for Teutonia, a German soccer team and I was playing for the Rovers, an Irish team. It was for the championship of the league and the winner would travel to Los Angeles for the State finals. This was the first year that my brother and I were on opposing teams. My family had to be on one side of the stadium for one half and the other side for the second half. The game ended in a tie and we had a shoot out, each team picked five players to shoot penalty kicks. Everyone on both teams had made the goals and there was only one kicker left. It was my brother. I asked the coach to put my in the goalie position because I knew it would play on my brother's mind. He shot and the ball went over the goal. We won and I lost a Brother for several months. It was not worth it.

2 Corinthians 4:16
Therefore we do not lose heart. Though outwardly we are wasting away, yet inwardly we are being renewed day by day.

Dan Says:
Sometime winning is the worst thing we can do.

# MOMENTS
## OF MINISTRY

# August 19

We were on the first site in Israel and as we walked down a path to a place where the ancient Israelis had built a altar I noticed an olive tree next to the path. I could not help myself as I said to my senior pastor "Jim there is an olive tree you have to taste one ". He reached up and plucked a nice big olive and placed it in his mouth. I had to laugh there is nothing as sour as the taste of a raw olive. He began to spit and sputter at the same time and the whole group was laughing as hard as we could. I had to remind Jim that I also had tasted an olive fresh off the tree that is how I knew what it tasted like. He laughed and from then on was very wary of any food products.

Ephesians 4:31
Get rid of all bitterness, rage and anger, brawling and slander, along with every form of malice.

Dan Says:
If only we could get rid of the bitterness in our heart and mind by spitting it out.

# MOMENTS
## OF MINISTRY

# August 20

My wife had a unique way of keeping me from driving her car. She had on the doors these great big daisies in living color. You could imagine if I showed up in the Police parking lot in that little rambler that looked as though it belonged to a hippie. But as things would have it my car broke down and I was forced to drive her car. I tried to sneak into the parking lot, but as luck would have it the Captain had an inspection of the troops. So everyone in the division saw me in the car. I knew after that if my car broke down again I was hitchhiking to work.

Ephesians 5:17
Therefore do not be foolish, but understand what the Lord's will is.

Dan Says:
Sometimes swallowing your pride tastes like a garbage can.

# Moments of Ministry

# August 21

The water was waist deep and the tunnel very narrow. It gave me a feeling of claustrophobia and, I wanted to get moving. I was in the lead with a flashlight and was speaking as I led the group through the tunnel that was carved by King Hezekiah many years ago. I could hear some grumbling behind me and was rethinking my decision to walk through. Just then I noticed a rat swimming toward us, I knew if the ladies saw it the panic would be overwhelming. I said in my loudest voice that everyone should look up and notice the comb chisel marks in the ceiling. They all complied and I breathed a sigh of relief as I realized that I was the only one to see the rat.

Matthew 18:10
See that you do not despise one of these little ones.

Dan Says:
Sometimes it is best just not to look and see.

# Moments
## of Ministry

# August 22

Louis Palou, a famous evangelist was coming to our area, and I was a member of the committee that had invited him to come. We had to make many plans for his stay and I was assigned to see he had security. I made arrangements with the Sherriff and he said that I was best qualified for the job. It was very interesting assignment for me. I would pick him up in the morning with a couple of his associates and make sure he got where he had to be at the right time. The thing the impressed me the most was all of the travel time with Mr. Palou he insisted that everyone in the car pray for whatever he was going to do next. No wonder he was so successful at his chosen profession.

Ephesians 6:18
And pray in the Spirit on all occasions with all kinds of prayers and requests.

Dan Says:
Who needs protection when you have prayer?

# MOMENTS
## OF MINISTRY

# August 23

The place was beautiful it was situated along a beautiful river and had plenty of space to park vehicles and put up tents. Our senior group had gone up for the weekend and we had a full slate of activities for everyone to participate in. One of the favorites was field golf where you place a tin pie plate on the ground and drive a stake through it. The distances vary with each hole and you are supposed to keep count of how many strokes it takes you to hit the plate. One thing I found out about seniors was they are lousy counters. Some of the scores could have won the U.S. Open that year. But the important thing was we had fun together.

James 3:2
We all stumble in many ways. Anyone who is never at fault in what they say is perfect, able to keep their whole body in check.

Dan Says:
True fellowship is impossible without an element of fun and joy.

# Moments of Ministry

# August 24

The dispatcher's voice was very disturbed as she was directing me to the parking lot of the State Police. Just as I was approaching the perimeter of the scene she came back on the air and said, "She is dead". I showed my badge to the officer at the scene and he let me cross the evidence tapes to get to where Linda was laying with a tarp over her body. I reported to the commanding officer and he asked if I would stay with him for a while. Soon we went inside to his office and he wanted to know what to do next. I told him we would have to make notification to next of kin and I saw the terror in his eyes, as the husband was also a trooper with the patrol. He asked if I would go with him and I said as long as we prayed first. He said that was the best idea he heard so for. He showed himself to be a real man of God during the notification to the husband and kids.

Luke 2:35
And a sword will pierce your own soul too.

Dan Says:
Courage comes in many ways, sometime it is in delivering a message.

# Moments
## of Ministry

# August 25

I had no doubt that my future son in law was in love with my daughter. I was going to baptize him in the river and it was snowing that day. He came right out to the deep water, seeing as how I was a Baptist I insisted that you go all the way under the water. My evil little mind said to hold him under till you get bubbles, but I didn't. We were both freezing and were actually blue when we came out of the river. This man was truly committed to my daughter. They have been married for many years now and he has grown in the Lord every year. His commitment to her and the Lord has never wavered in the least.

Proverbs 25:25
Like cold water to a weary soul is good news from a distant land.

Dan Says:
When you decide to go, go all the way.


# Moments of Ministry

# August 26

It was at least 125 degrees in there and I was struggling as hard as I could. In my hand were several metal rods and the canvas were collapsing on me and I was getting angrier by the minute. It was one of those times you could count on leading to an argument with my wife. The tent was a torture instrument that was always guaranteed to get my temper to a point that I would lose it at everyone and everything. The Bedouin in the Middle East had it right, they had the women put up the tent while they sat in the shade and guarded them for any enemy.

Isaiah 54:2
Enlarge the place of your tent, stretch your tent curtains wide, do not hold back;

Dan Says:
Pray before those annual fights, Tents in summer, and then the Christmas tree.

# Moments
## of Ministry

## August 27

We were in the Garden Tomb complex in Israel and we had just looked at Golgotha and now we walked to the tomb of Jesus. It was a very moving experience and I never saw anyone who was not touched emotionally by this place. Earlier, all the pastors had decided that our senior pastor would do a communion service at this place. When the elements came and it was time to talk, Jim, our senior pastor was unable to speak. He just looked at me and I knew that I had to fill in for him. It was a wonderful thing to see that our pastor was so touched by this place that he truly loved and worshipped Jesus as we are all supposed too.

Psalm 95:6
Come, let us bow down in worship, let us kneel before the Lord our Maker;

Dan Says:
Sometime worship is not being able to speak.

# MOMENTS
## OF MINISTRY

# August 28

Over the Allenby Bridge into Israel for the first time, I was surprised to see the explosives in plain sight on the bridge. Having been on the bomb squad I recognized the satchel charges and saw that the border was heavily guarded by troops with weapons at the ready. You can imagine my surprise when my foot first touched the soil of Israel I felt like I had come home. The questioning that we went through was very efficient and handled with great care. What a problem for the Israelis they wanted people to come to the land, but had to be careful not to let in terrorists who wanted to bring harm. The young army officer who interrogated me was really good; she asked how I knew what an explosive charge was. Someone on the bus heard me tell my wife what they were and told the guards.

Deuteronomy 33:12
"Let the beloved of the Lord rest secure in him, for he shields him all day long, and the one the Lord loves rests between his shoulders."

Dan Says:
God protects, but you have to do your part.

# Moments of Ministry

# August 29

Tackling him to the ground the fight heated up. I finally got a good pressure hold on him and he was in too much pain to resist any longer. I placed the handcuffs on him and he just started screaming how I was hurting him. Soon there were a lot of people on the street and he continued to holler that I was picking on him because he was black. It was just as the riots in Los Angeles were starting and the people between my car and us were all black. There was some yelling starting about taking my prisoner. I pulled my revolver and placed it under his chin and asked him to tell them to let us get to the car. He complied and the crowd hesitated long enough for us to get into the car before they charged us. I was able to escape with him, but the car suffered lot of damage.

Psalm 91:2
I will say of the Lord, "He is my refuge and my fortress, my God, in whom I trust."

Dan Says:
Never surrender to evil.

# Moments of Ministry

# August 30

The bear rug that hangs over our fireplace fascinates my dog. Every once in a while he goes over to give it a good smell and try to determine if it is real or not. He then comes and decides that maybe he should get into my lap just in case. He is a boxer and weighs about eighty pounds and is all muscle. I just love to see how his mind works and the process of his thinking. I believe that John the dog thinks that the bear will protect him when we are gone. He is smarter than you think because he knows that there is something that is bigger and smarter than him that is able to provide protection. I wish sometimes I were smart enough to remember that there is someone that is bigger and smarter than me who always provides protection. I just have to ask.

Psalm 5:1
Listen to my words, Lord, consider my lament.

Dan Says:
Remember who your protector is always.

# Moments of Ministry

# August 31

Lying on the sandy beach catching some rays the man seemed very at peace with himself, by the time I arrived he looked much different. How could a guy get run over while lying on a sandy beach I wondered? And then I saw the vehicle that did it, a jet ski. Someone who was devoid of any brains had let a little boy drive the ski do. He panicked and thought that he was doing right by heading for shore. Apparently he was going at such speed that he drove several yards onto the shore. I guess it was a good thing I was Chaplain, as I would have arrested the father and booked him for manslaughter. The officers in charge had a conference among them and issued a citation. I felt the most sorrow for the child.

Proverbs 16:25
There is a way that appears to be right, but in the end it leads to death.

Dan Says:
Common sense is acquired by a lifetime of making good decisions.

# Moments of Ministry

# September 1

The water in Poipu was warm and wonderful the little bay we were swimming in was loaded with all kinds of colorful fish. My wife and I were snorkeling and having a great time. Occasionally one of us would say come over here the fish are all over the place. As we were going along enjoying ourselves we both at the same time spotted the huge shadow coming by us. I think we broke all Olympic swimming records as we headed for the beach. Once safely on the shore we saw the denizen of the deep it was a monk seal that was coming to shore to sun itself. The thought that went through both of our minds was SHARK. I am glad we were wrong, and it nice to know that we can really swim fast if we have to.

Micah 2:10
Get up, go away! For this is not your resting place,

Dan Says:
Fear can be good if it is God you fear in reverence.

# Moments of Ministry

# September 2

Barbara Simpson sat in front of me when I attended Most Holy Redeemer Catholic School. She was a brat and a tattletale and always enjoyed getting me in trouble. Our desks in those days had inkwells and we used pens that had a nub on them that was changeable. We also wore little uniforms. Boys wore a white shirt, a blue tie and cords. Girls wore little sailor outfits that were white. One day after Barbra got me in trouble again I could not resist. I reached forward and got her long pigtail and dipped in into the inkwell. Her uniform was ruined and she went into a crying fit that deserved an academy award. The school had enough of me and asked my parents to enroll me in public school. It might have been the best thing that ever happened to me.

Romans 8:28
And we know that in all things God works for the good of those who love him, who have been called according to his purpose.

Dan Says:
Look carefully sometimes you are in the wrong place.

# MOMENTS OF MINISTRY

# September 3

Somebody told me that corndogs were invented in San Francisco at the Cliff House, which overlooks the Pacific Ocean. I do not know if that was true, but I do know that I loved them. Now in order to get them when I was on duty I had to go through four different police districts to get to them. I had to make sure that I was not spotted by other district police cars as that would be infringing on their eating areas, once I was caught by a patrol car and had to promise that I would bring them special sandwiches that were only made in my police district. Now you would think that the police would have more important things to do. We did, but those corndogs were too good to resist.

1 Corinthians 10:13
No temptation has overtaken you except what is common to mankind. And God is faithful; he will not let you be tempted beyond what you can bear.

Dan Says:
What you are not supposed to have is always the best.

# Moments
## of Ministry

## September 4

Both of us were retired; he a retired army officer and I a retired cop. We found that we had a lot in common and soon became the best of friends. As couples we traveled and went places and did a variety of things. Once in a conversation it came up that Sam had a Rolex watch he kept in a drawer at home I said if I had a Rolex I would sure wear it. As Sam aged he became sicker and was sure he did not have a lot of time left. He invited me and my wife to lunch and with great ceremony presented me with the watch. He said I would appreciate the watch and if he left it to the kids they would just sell it. I wore the watch proudly for several months and would often have to explain how a preacher could afford a Rolex. Now it sits in a drawer and I have to decide who I want to have the watch.

Matthew 10:8
...Freely you have received; freely give.

Dan Says:
Though the gift was good, the thought behind it was greater.

# Moments of Ministry

## September 5

Right after the round of golf the patron said he would contact me at the caddy shack when he had any news for me. I had carried his bag for eighteen holes and when he was finished I brought the bag to locker room after I had cleaned the clubs. It was during the round of golf that I heard him say to his playing partner that he needed one more fighter for the club matches that Friday night. I told him I was in training with Dick Lagrille a pretty famous trainer in San Francisco. The word came and I was to fight on the next card. Dick told me I was not ready for that caliber of fight, but I insisted that I was. I lost by TKO in first round. I was way out classed and learned a good lesson. Listen to the experts they really know best.

1 Peter 1:13
Therefore, with minds that are alert and fully sober, set your hope on the grace to be brought to you when Jesus Christ is revealed at his coming.

Dan Says:
Listen to those who have your best interest at heart.

# MOMENTS OF MINISTRY

# September 6

Camp was all set up and we decided to eat, when I went to the pick-up I could not find the food. I asked my brother in law where he put the food and he said that I was supposed to put the food in. My pick up had three gas tanks on it so we were as far as we could get from any store. Fortunately I had my fishing gear with me. And though it was not in season we had to fish for food. I was one of those fishermen who put back all fish I caught, but this was different. We ate fish that would normally be big enough for bait. One truck came by our camp and we asked if we could buy some food he was on his way home so he said we could have what he had. It was canned spaghetti and beans. I never tasted anything so good.

Hebrews 13:2
Do not forget to show hospitality to strangers, for by so doing some people have shown hospitality to angels without knowing it.

Dan Says:
Them boy scouts have it right; Be Prepared.

# MOMENTS OF MINISTRY

# September 7

The waitress just brought our food; we were having a food adventure with some friends. Someone had given me a certificate for Thai food and we were redeeming it at the restaurant. I felt adventurous and ordered something I had never tasted before. The waitress set down my plate and said the noodles were black because they were dyed with squid ink. My first thought was to just eat the shrimp and pass on the noodles, but being raised never to waste food I began to eat them. It was a lot like I imagined fire eating would taste like. We finished our meal with a wonderful desert so it was worthwhile. The fellowship was really the best part of all.

Colossians 3:1
Since, then, you have been raised with Christ, set your hearts on things above, where Christ is, seated at the right hand of God.

Dan Says:
Great taste does not always have to do with food.

# Moments
## of Ministry

# September 8

Standing on the platform looking at the rope that crossed over the river I thought maybe this zip line was not a good idea. But then I decided that I would go first and get it over with. As they were putting me in the gear for the ride I overheard a young man with us say that there was no way he would do the zip line. Then my wife who was over seventy said how much she was looking forward to doing it. The shame was more than the young man could stand so he went on the line. It made me think that if we all had the courage to do things that do not seem comfortable how much more enjoyment we would have in this life.

Joshua 10:25
Joshua said to them, "Do not be afraid; do not be discouraged. Be strong and courageous.

Dan Says:
Sometimes courage is just lack of fear.

# Moments of Ministry

# September 9

When you join the navy there is a very real loss of freedom. There is always someone telling you what to do, how to do it and when you are to do it. As bad as that is imagine being in the brig in the service where there is even less freedom. I ended up here because I had made a promise to take my girlfriend to the prom. The navy said I could not go, but I said yes I can. When I came back from being "over the hill" or absent without leave. I was court-martialed and sent to the brig. Along with loss of pay, it was a hard time for me. I can say I did not like it, but was it worth it? YES!!!

Leviticus 18:4
You must obey my laws and be careful to follow my decrees. I am the Lord your God.

Dan Says:
If you want to have your own way, you must be willing to pay the cost.

# Moments of Ministry

# September 10

A farmer in the valley was having a real hard time with rabbits in his fields. He came up with the idea to have police come and shoot the rabbits. He would provide the ammunition and also give us a great lunch. We jumped at the chance to practice shooting at moving targets. I had just come back from the police Olympics and had won the gold medal in archery. All the guys said show us how good you are with the bow on moving targets. I strung the bow and spotted a rabbit way out there. I snapped off a shot with no hope of even coming close. The arrow flew like it had eyes and nailed the rabbit right through the neck. I could take that shot a thousand times and never make it. However, I unstrung my bow like I just made another shot and they were amazed.

Hebrews 12:12
Therefore, strengthen your feeble arms and weak knees.

Dan Says:
When a miracle happens, shut up and accept it.

# MOMENTS OF MINISTRY

# September 11

We were getting ready to leave Israel and the guide said to everyone "be sure they do not stamp your passport, we are going into Egypt ". As my wife came up to passport control the agent asked, "Do you want your passport stamped" and she said "yes". We got into Egypt with no problem and as we were going to Greece next I was not too worried. But, our plane had trouble and we had to set down in Syria. Syrians were death on anything Jewish. The plane never left the tarmac and we had to keep all window shades down. Was I ever happy when the plane finally took off. God really protected us and we knew it was because of Him.

Song of Songs 1:4
We rejoice and delight in you; we will praise your love more than wine.

Dan Says:
God is always there when we need Him.

# Moments
## of Ministry

## September 12

We finally got a car. It was not much to look at, but it ran and got us where we wanted to go. The car was parked on the street outside our little apartment; we lived on the steepest street in the city, the police trained their motorcycle riders there. As we were eating one night there was a terrible crash outside. When we came out there was a car that had hit a car further up the street and that car had turned over and hit our car. We only had the minimum insurance on our auto. We insured the other guy not us. Not so with the car that hit us, it was owned by an unemployed pants presser with no money. So much for our transportation now it was back on the bus until we could save for another car.

Habakkuk 3:16
I heard and my heart pounded, my lips quivered at the sound;

Dan Says:
Sometimes you can't get ahead no matter what you do, enjoy it anyway.

# Moments
## of Ministry

# September 13

The people who lived across the street came pounding on our door. You have a chimney fire they yelled, they said they had already called the fire department and they were on the way. We got out the dogs and tied them to the car bumper and the firemen arrived. They asked if we had everybody out and we said yes. As they were putting out the fire my son in laws brother came out of the house in his bathrobe. We had forgotten he was staying downstairs, the fireman asked if there was anyone else and we said no. He said that he was going to check just in case. He gave us a very strange look and I certainly didn't blame him.

Luke 12:6
Yet not one of them is forgotten by God.

Dan Says:
When in panic mode, stop pray and remember to think clearly.

# Moments
## of Ministry

## September 14

My wife had taken a whole bunch of girl scouts on an outing in our Toyota Land Cruiser Toyota. As they were coming home from the ocean and heading up a big hill the car started to run badly and finally stop altogether. A gentleman stopped to help her and when he raised the hood of the car found the problem right away. The rotor cap had lost one of its metal clips that hold the cap in place. The man told my wife there was nothing he could do. Never underestimate the thinking power of girl scouts. They got the car running and when she pulled in a garage the mechanic called to all his buddies to come and look. My wife had fixed the cap by placing a Band-Aid on it. They all roared laughing at the fix.

1 Samuel 12:23
…And I will teach you the way that is good and right.

Dan Says:
Girl Scout saying "Be Prepared" can take a problem solving to a new height.

# Moments
## of Ministry

# September 15

For two years I had taught the early morning Bible study at church. It was a fun group that met every week and we always came prepared. I liked to bring a lollipop to the class and the person who asked the best question or made the best statement would get the sucker. As time went on the class grew so much it filled the room. There was one man who sat in the front every week and took notes. One day during class this gentleman looked up at me and asked, "Do you mean to tell me that Jesus was God?" I could not believe it. I asked myself what in the world was I teaching that this question even arose. I learned from that point in my teaching about the Bible to "Put the cookies on the bottom shelf", in other words keep the teaching simple. He got the lollipop for his great discovery.

Psalm 119:130
The unfolding of your words gives light; it gives understanding to the simple.

Dan Says:
Do not assume that everyone understands everything you say.

# Moments of Ministry

## September 16

He was back at work at the greyhound bus station I had arrested him several time for his scams that he would use to fleece people from their money. He did not see me as I approached him from the rear. I got to hear the whole tale he was giving to this businessman who was waiting to commute home from his job. He was saying that he had to get to New York as his mother was very sick. The victim said he could give him five dollars, but Slick said no he did not want charity, but he did have a very rare gold piece that he would make a deal on. The gold piece was carefully placed in a plastic holder and looked very real. The man agreed to buy the piece for one hundred dollars, and then I stepped in and said around the corner he could buy the same piece for fifty cents. He was really angry and wanted Slick arrested. I asked him "what for?' you agreed to buy. I sent both on their way with a stern warning.

>1 Timothy 6:10
>For the love of money is a root of all kinds of evil.

Dan Says:
Do not get fooled by the packaging, look at the product.

# Moments
## of Ministry

# September 17

There he is sitting on a chair with his chin on the window sill looking out at the world. I am sitting at my desk writing and he is just keeping me company. I know that God has provided this wonderful friend for me. I love to be with John and he loves to be with me. He comes and wakes my every morning with a kiss and then we play for a few minutes. He is always there to hear my deepest fears and he seems to understand. Even though he weighs over eighty pounds he loves to sit in my lap and just relax. He does not ask much of me but he constantly wants to bring me joy. I have had many dogs in my life, but none like John. He wants to be with me just because he loves me, no conditions just love. I want to love Jesus like John love me.

1 Peter 1:22
Now that you have purified yourselves by obeying the truth so that you have sincere love for each other, love one another deeply, from the heart.

Dan Says:
Sometimes love is just being there.

# Moments of Ministry

# September 18

At my small group meeting last night we had our pastor show up with his wife. It was interesting to see Greg checking up on me as my leader. You see I remember him when he came on staff as a man who worked at the lumber mill as a saw filer. He attended all the classes that I taught at the church so that he could be ordained as a minister of the gospel. The thing I enjoyed most about him was that he completely sold out to being a man of God. He was now a seasoned pastor who had been through many of the trials that young pastors go through and he was still as sold out as he was in the start of his ministry experience. I know I should not, but I am very proud of my young men in ministry.

2 Timothy 4:5
But you, keep your head in all situations, endure hardship, do the work of an evangelist, discharge all the duties of your ministry.

Dan Says:
It is great to look back and love what you did.

# MOMENTS
## OF MINISTRY

# September 19

Being an old guy, when it snows my neighbors always come to my aid and help when the snow falls. I have one neighbor with a four-wheeler that has a blade in front and he does a great job for me. I do however keep the walk from the door to the driveway clean myself. We had an especially bad year of snow and then freezing weather so that a lot of ice had formed. Soon the driveway and the street in front of the mailbox were cleared of snow. I started to walk out to thank everyone when all of a sudden I saw my feet go up in front of my face. I remember thinking this is not going to end well. I was very lucky as I landed on the hardest thing I had, my head. A trip to the hospital revealed that I only had a very sore neck. But I sure scared a lot of people.

2 Samuel 1:19
"A gazelle lies slain on your heights, Israel. How the mighty have fallen!

Dan Says:
A fall to remember is not always physical.

# Moments
## of Ministry

# September 20

When the call came to dispatch I was standing there one of the dispatchers motioned for me to come to her station. She was talking to a woman who was threatening suicide. We told her that I was going to come to her house to talk with her. When I arrived she explained that she did not have the money to send to her son who was in debt to some dope dealers. I told her that she could never get her son out of trouble if she continued to bail him out. She asked what could she do and I explained that the only thing that could save her son was a Savior and explained that she should have him contact a pastor and get right with God and then he could live a normal life. She asked how could that help and I had the opportunity to lead her to the Lord. I said she should tell someone and when she called a friend even where I was sitting I heard "Praise the lord ". I knew she was in good hands.

Proverbs 18:10
The name of the Lord is a fortified tower; the righteous run to it and are safe.

Dan Says:
Save yourself and then you will be able to save others.

# Moments of Ministry

# September 21

We were driving by the main post office while all the employees were having lunch. It was the late shift and they seemed to dislike us because there were many shouts of derision and a lot of cussing. They really enjoy themselves calling us names and giving us the one finger salute. My partner was busy looking at the California vehicle code and suddenly he gave me a great big smile. It seems that all autos must be parked at least eight feet from railroad tracks. After the crowd went inside we measured and sure enough they were parked six feet away. After towing thirty cars, we went to lunch very happy police officers.

Proverbs 22:28
Do not move an ancient boundary stone set up by your ancestors.

Dan Says:
It can be fun to twist the tail of the tiger, until it bites.

# Moments of Ministry

# September 22

My grandson was talking to his friends and was not aware that I could hear him. He was telling them that they could have a lot of fun watching me lose my temper. He began to explain to them that whenever I heard the name Jane Fonda I would explode in a fit of anger. He would have been right most of the time because I had a great dislike for that particular person, because she acted as a traitor during the war. She posed with the enemy and gave them great comfort and publicity. I simply regarded her as a traitor and as such had a very low opinion of her. I know she later recanted and said she was sorry, but that came way too late for me. I did not lose my temper with the kids, but they got a real lesson in patriotism.

James 5:17
If anyone, then, knows the good they ought to do and doesn't do it, it is sin for them.

Dan Says:
Your actions will follow you all your life.

# Moments of Ministry

# September 23

Even the hotel we stayed at in Athens had statues in the lobby. Everywhere we went in the city there were statues of nude men doing everything possible. Right outside our hotel room door was a statue that was endowed way too much. My wife finally said that she was going to take a sheet out of our room and give the poor gentleman a toga to wear. I asked her please do not do that as we were hated enough by the Greeks because of the war in Kosovo. I had given instructions to people on the tour if you were asked where you were from say Canada. I can say that it was embarrassing for me also to see all these nude statues.

Acts 17:16
While Paul was waiting for them in Athens, he was greatly distressed to see that the city was full of idols.

Dan Says:
There is a difference between art and pornography, it is called clothes.

# Moments of Ministry

## September 24

On our way to the campground we stopped at a country store to get some supplies. We continued on and when we arrived at our campsite we decided that we would have the canned chicken we purchased at the store. Well one look at what came out of the can was enough for us to decide that we had better go to town for dinner. It always surprises me that what is on the picture on the outside of the package is not even close to what is really inside. Kind of like some churches they really look good on the outside, but once you see what they are about they really stink.

2 Corinthians 11; 13
For such people are false apostles, deceitful workers, masquerading as apostles of Christ.

Dan Says:
Some bad stuff even smells good.

# Moments
## of Ministry

# September 25

Unable to resist I asked the women on the tour if they had to use the rest room. I have never asked that question without having someone say they needed the facilities. This time I asked on the temple mount and I knew what to expect. The ladies entered the rest area and saw a lady who was selling toilet paper for a shekel a square. If they did buy and decided to use the toilet they discovered a hole in the ground and nothing else. When they came out some were angry while others were laughing at the experience. I have found that when you encounter a new experience that is uncomfortable you should go with the flow.

Philippians 4:4
Rejoice in the Lord always. I will say it again: Rejoice!

Dan Says:
Sometimes it is not about your comfort.

# Moments
## of Ministry

## September 26

I had gotten the car of my dreams a Ford Thunderbird convertible. I really loved that car and drove it with great pride wherever I went. It was black with a red interior, a real eye catcher. My wife and kids wanted to do something nice for me so they decided to wash my car. I knew something was wrong as soon as I entered the room. All three looked as if someone had just passed away. I finally asked what happened and my wife said that she and the girls were doing something nice when the accident happened. My wife left the door open as she backed out of the carport. The door sustained substantial damage and even the fender was crumpled. The worst part was I had to drive my wife's car with the daisy on the door, while it was being fixed.

Isaiah 22:4
Therefore I said, "Turn away from me; let me weep bitterly.

Dan Says:
Things are just things.

# Moments of Ministry

# September 27

The chef smiled broadly and said that today was very special he had gotten some very special treats from his supplier. He was the sushi chef and he always wanted to please me. I did not have the heart to tell him I did not care for raw fish, so I made up a story that I was not allowed to eat at an outside stand. So he always gave me my treat in a white box. I could always find kids down the street that were very happy to have the box and keep my secret. One day I came and he handed me a white box and I accepted it gratefully. He said open please and when I did there was a cheeseburger. He said I do not know how you can eat that junk and laughed. He had known for some time and said he did not mind feeding the children. What a wonderful beat to walk, such generous people.

Matthew 10:8
… Freely you have received; freely give.

Dan Says:
There is no waste in a gift given in love.

# Moments
## of Ministry

## September 28

I love to collect old golf stories and one of my favorites took place at Royal St. Georges at Sandwich England. They had a very strict policy that banned women from the course. This policy became a real problem when a team from Cambridge University came to play a match. On their team was a woman golfer named Fiona. They had an emergency meeting of the committee for rules and procedures and attempted to come up with a ruling that all would be satisfied with. They finally came up with a solution they named Fiona an honorary man. Sounds like us when we do not like the rules of the Bible; we just call a meeting and figure a way around them.

Proverbs 16:25
There is a way that appears to be right, but in the end it leads to death.

Dan Says:
God says what He means and means what He says.

# MOMENTS OF MINISTRY

# September 29

There was a town in northern California called Occidental; it was famous for the food served in two restaurants. They were the only places to eat in town and had a fierce competition over what they served. Both places only served steak or duck so the real competition came in the food that came before the main dish. The antipasto plate was full of great selections of cheese meats and vegetables. Next the most delicious soup you ever had, served family style in a large bowl. Then the salad course with olives, tomatoes, peppers, and everything you could imagine. After all that we could never eat our main course and always brought it home in a box. It was never as good reheated but that was always the way it was.

Psalm 145:7
They celebrate your abundant goodness and joyfully sing of your righteousness.

Dan Says:
We constantly have to realize to keep the main thing the main thing.

# Moments
## of Ministry

## September 30

Here I was again walking down the center of the carpenter's union hall with a can of air freshener in each hand trying my best to eliminate the odors in this place. I had told myself no more church plants after the first one. It was in an abandoned dairy barn. Talk about stink we had to shovel manure out of that building and it was really a chore. The church we planted in a factory smelled like oil all the time and the one in a round house also presented unique problems. But when you look back there were fond memories of those little churches. Now The Lord was gracious to me as the last several years I have been in a large church, but we went from a movie theatre to two schools before getting our first building. Growing in the ministry is not always easy, but always rewarding.

James 5:8
You too, be patient and stand firm, because the Lord's coming is near.

Dan Says:
When you get near the finish, run harder.

# MOMENTS OF MINISTRY

# October 1

John suffers from separation anxiety and will cause great damage when we leave him alone in the house. He is getting better all the time but still suffers setbacks occasionally. At first he would tear down the curtains in the front room, but finally got over that. He does however seem to know what you consider precious and go for those items. He has ruined two kindle readers and a pair of my wife's glasses. We learned if we left the radio on he was better. Funny though if we left rock and roll he was destructive, but if we had a preacher station on he was good. I guess we have a Christian Boxer dog after all.

1 Corinthians 13:4
Love is patient, love is kind. It does not envy, it does not boast, it is not proud.

Dan Says:
When you decide to love, do it unconditionally.

# Moments
## of Ministry

# October 2

I left for the headquarters as soon as I heard the news. I was on a hunt for a inspector in the intelligence department of the police department. When I went into the office and asked for him the receptionist told me he had gone to lunch. I asked where and when she said a restaurant on my beat I was very pleased. I had played football with this inspector in high school and so I thought we were friends. His name was Mike and when I got to the restaurant he was just exiting. I walked up to him and knocked him down with a good right hand punch. He asked what was wrong and I told him about the man we ran a check on from our car and communication was told to tell us he was clear. Later we found out he was a cop killer from Chicago and intelligence was following him around. I said I did not care when someone is dangerous I want to know.

Proverbs 28:26
Those who trust in themselves are fools, but those who walk in wisdom are kept safe.

Dan Says:
With friends trust is a must.

# Moments of Ministry

# October 3

My girls were always working on some kind of badge for their Girl Scouts. Though their mother was the best source for learning the skills for becoming a good girl scout, occasionally I could be of some help. One time when we were camping the girls had to observe and record an insect doing whatever insects do. Well one time sure enough a mosquito landed on me, I quickly called for the girls to come over and observe the insect bite me. They carefully watched as it stung me and seemed to know I would not kill it. So it drank and drank my blood. It flew away quite satisfied and the girls walked away to make their notes. I scratched the itch for two days.

1 Peter 3:13
Who is going to harm you if you are eager to do good?

Dan Says:
The best gifts sometime cost you nothing.

# MOMENTS OF MINISTRY

# October 4

When our church was smaller, one of my duties was to meet/counsel with couples. I being an old retired cop was not known for my compassion. They made a rule that you could only counsel a couple four times. I very rarely had a couple come back for the second time. I would try to listen and be compassionate but I would always come back to the same solution for every problem. I would say what the Bible says about that. It seemed that they never wanted to hear that. Once I heard one couple plea with the front office please give us Charlie; anybody but Dan. You know the people that I did counsel with almost always stayed together. I guess the Bible knows best.

1 Peter 4:1
Therefore, since Christ suffered in his body, arm yourselves also with the same attitude, because whoever suffers in the body is done with sin.

Dan Says:
The truth hurts, but it heals.

# Moments of Ministry

# October 5

When I retired on a disability from the police department I was surprised that the city was paying me for my accrued sick time I had not used. It was quite a bit of money so we decided to do something that we could not afford. We took our family to Disneyland and brought a friend of the kids who needed a wheel chair to see the park. While eating lunch the three little pigs came by and one of them knocked off my hat and got a big laugh. Well he knocked off my hat a second time and I told him no more. He just had to do it again and that was when I said if he did it again he was going to be bacon. I looked over and some hippies had taken our wheel chair and were trying to get away. I caught up with them and during the confrontation I got pretty loud. A passing woman said" is that the same guy who was picking on the pig"? There was no way I could win in that place.

Hebrews 13:18
Pray for us. We are sure that we have a clear conscience and desire to live honorably in every way.

Dan Says:
Sometimes you look bad doing good.

# Moments of Ministry

# October 6

Even though it was sold out for three years in advance my daughter said lets try to get tickets. The play was My Fair Lady at the Royal Theatre on Drury Lane in London. Well it was right after the September eleventh bombing and international travel was way down. We did get tickets though we could not sit with each other. I was in the very last row of seats in the theatre it was so high and far from the stage that I saw the play through the chandeliers in the theatre. The worst part was when we arrived we tried to go through the front doors and were turned back by a doorman who said in a snotty voice you have to enter through the side door. The play was truly wonderful but the doorman was a twit.

2 Corinthians 6:17
Therefore, "Come out from them and be separate, says the Lord.

Dan Says:
When people look down on you, He is looking down at them.

# Moments
## of Ministry

# October 7

The convertible was traveling very slowly down the street and it was my turn. I threw the water balloon in a perfect arc and it was beautiful to behold. The lady sitting next to the driver got it right on top of her head. We were laughing as hard as we could when suddenly the car stopped and the man who was driving came running toward us. We were off like a flash but this guy was really fast and really angry. He seemed to be intent on catching me in particular. He must have seen me throw the balloon. I took this guy through blackberry patches, over fences and through alleys. He just would not give up. Finally I went into the basement of the old apartments, which had dozens of storerooms and other places to hide. I heard him search for a while and give up. But I hope I never meet that guy even now.

Proverbs 6:33
Blows and disgrace are his lot, and his shame will never be wiped away.

Dan Says:
I am truly sorry now, but so happy he did not catch me.

# Moments of Ministry

# October 8

Like any good beat cop I was standing in a darkened doorway watching what was going on. I spotted this guy who was very popular with all kinds of people. At least a dozen people had come up to him and had exchanged something with him. It was obvious to me he was dealing. He seemed to be out of product and started to walk away. I decided to follow him and he went into a cheap hotel down the street. I asked the desk clerk what room he was in and he told me. I went to the door and knocked I heard him say come in. I was sure he was not expecting me but I obliged anyway. There on the table were all kind of balloons and weighing scales. I had hit the jackpot. I arrested him and called for a narcotic team to help me process the drugs. While I was waiting for them his partner came in with more drugs and cash. Sometimes it's just too good to imagine.

1 John 1:5
This is the message we have heard from him and declare to you: God is light; in him there is no darkness at all.

Dan Says:
Stay in the light and you will be all right. It's where He lives and plays.

# Moments
## of Ministry

# October 9

While in Victoria British Columba my wife had decided that we must go to the famous Butchart Gardens. I had to admit that the flowers were beautiful and the grounds were perfect in every sense. After we had walked for a long time we were famished and had to get something to eat. We found a teahouse and the ladies wanted to go there. I was outnumbered and had no choice so I agreed. Now I am a hamburger type of guy and this was way out of my comfort zone. The food finally arrived and they were tiny sandwiches, hardly even a bite. I grabbed one and placed it in my mouth and then the taste hit me. My wife looked at me and said very firmly "do not spit that out ". I got it down but I went away very hungry.

Mark 2:23
One Sabbath Jesus was going through the grain fields, and as his disciples walked along, they began to pick some heads of grain.

Dan Says:
When traveling, a wise man carries a Snickers at all times.

# MOMENTS OF MINISTRY

# October 10

My Son-in-law Bob and I wanted to play a golf course on the island where we were staying. My daughter got us starting times on the course and made arrangements to rent clubs. When we arrived at the course I asked Bob if he wanted a souvenir of the course. He said no but I bought a tee shirt that said KO'OLAU the world's hardest golf course. I thought that's a very strange thing to put on a shirt. But I soon found out that it was true as far as I was concerned. I lost seven balls on the first nine holes. It was like driving golf balls down a hallway. To make it worse there was jungle on each hole. I hit one into the jungle and went to see if I could find the ball. All I saw were something that looked like the world's biggest rats. They could have the ball.

1 Corinthians 10:23
"I have the right to do anything"—but not everything is constructive.

Dan Says:
If they advertise the worst and you buy, shame on you.

# MOMENTS OF MINISTRY

# October 11

We were on his heels the alarm went off and we were just a block away. He was on foot and our car had him in the spotlight so he was all ours. The place he ran to was a warehouse area and he ran up a loading ramp with us right on his tail. I was very surprised to find that he suddenly just disappeared from sight. The realization came at us very fast the ramp had run out and he simply jumped off the end. As our speed was excessive we found ourselves airborne and flying at least five feet off the ground. When we landed it was evident that the car part of the chase was over. The car sustained major damage and I was as mad as I have ever been. I had been suckered into five hours of damage reports as well as a lot of ridicule from the tow driver to every cop in the district. I hope the guy we were pursuing was caught later.

Proverbs 28:26
Those who trust in themselves are fools, but those who walk in wisdom are kept safe.

Dan Says:
The winner of the race is not always the fastest.

# Moments of Ministry

# October 12

It was a good thing that we were moving out of town. One more bite and our dog Valiant was going to be put to sleep. We had a whole new county to use up his bites. He was a German shepherd mix and was the meanest dog I ever saw. He would sneak up on people and bite them with no warning at all. When I brought my police dog Shelby home I was a little worried about Valiant, but I did not need to. It came as a surprise that my mongrel would beat up the much bigger police dog. I had to build a fence down the middle of the yard to protect the police dog. I bet my personal dog would have been the better police dog.

2 Timothy 3:1
But mark this: There will be terrible times in the last days.

Dan Says:
It is not how you look, but how you act.

# Moments
## of Ministry

# October 13

The super sergeant came up with a really good idea and asked if the captain would approve. The captain did not even ask what the idea was because he had such great trust in the sergeant. Our problem at every demonstration was the same. The agitators and instigators were never in front at the demonstration they always had the poor suckers up front who would take the brunt of our charge when we advanced on the crowd. So one time we had several guys in plain clothes with lead loaded leather saps planted in the crowd. One minute before the squads were to advance on the demonstrators we put down most of the real troublemakers. They beat us in court, but boy was it worth it.

John 16:16
"In a little while you will see me no more, and then after a little while you will see me."

Dan Says:
It is true you can hide in a crowd.

# Moments
## of Ministry

# October 14

I guess that there is a fine line between courage and stupidity. I had just come from the emergency hospital by the docks where I was given a hot bath to get my body temperature back to where it belongs. He called me into his office and asked what I was thinking. I had jumped into the bay to help a man who was struggling in the water. I took off my belt and shoes and went in to help him. There were a lot of things floating by that normally would have made me sick. There was no ladder so I brought him to the pier and we held on to poles that held the pier up. It took many minutes for the fireboat to get to us and we were exhausted. We had to go to the hospital right away.

The Captain said I was stupid for jumping in the water, and then he put me up for a medal.

Psalm 91:3
Surely he will save you from the fowler's snare and from the deadly pestilence.

Dan Says:
I guess you can be courageous and stupid at the same time.

# Moments of Ministry

# October 15

I opened the door of my hotel room in Honolulu and picked up the paper. I always enjoyed a morning cup of coffee and the paper on the deck of the hotel room while I waited for my wife to get dressed and ready for the day's events. I noticed that it was not the local paper we had always received before but the U.S.A. newspaper. We then went down to the beach for a morning swim and I noticed there were not as many people as usual. We were sunning ourselves when I noticed a policeman come by. He was wearing plastic booties over his shoes. I asked what that was about and found out there was a sewage leak into the beach area. Now I bought a local paper and there read all about the horrible leak. I have never gone back to Oahu since.

> James 1:16
> Don't be deceived, my dear brothers and sisters.

> Dan Says:
> Not telling can be as bad as lying.

# MOMENTS OF MINISTRY

# October 16

One of the really sad parts of being a police officer are the people you come in contact with that have mental disabilities. They, through no fault of their own often end up on the wrong side of the law. I remember one gentleman who came into an all you could eat establishment and was on his second tray of chicken when the owner called us and wanted him arrested. I explained to the proprietor that when he said all you could eat that was what was allowed for the customer. I was able to strike a bargain with both by saying you could not just eat one thing. Everyone was happy after that. The gentleman who was the eater was always easy to recognize as he wore a tin foil hat everywhere he went.

James 1:27
Religion that God our Father accepts as pure and faultless is this: to look after orphans and widows in their distress and to keep oneself from being polluted by the world.

Dan Says:
I KNOW God really cares for those who cannot care for themselves.

# Moments
## of Ministry

# October 17

There is no way we are selling you a raffle ticket this year. That is what the sergeant told me when it was time to buy the tickets for the widows and orphans raffle. I had won the first prize two years in a row and everyone was angry with me for winning. I said that is was all right as I already had two diamond rings. Instead I entered a raffle for one of the officers who was a member of a fraternal organization and would you believe it I won a set of golf clubs. Now I can't help it if I am lucky I think it comes with being Irish or something. But the best thing that ever happened in my life had nothing to do with luck; it was a conscious decision to follow Jesus.

1 Corinthians 10:24
No one should seek their own good, but the good of others.

Dan Says:
We get to give, not give to get.

# Moments of Ministry

# October 18

Swimming in the river is a lot of fun and we do a lot every year. One time the whole family was down at the river and we decided to swim across the river. We had all gotten across and while on the return my wife suddenly found that she was in trouble and was not sure if she could make it back. Our dog Fuzzy a lab saw her problem and immediately swam to her. She got a hold of the dog's tail and was towed to safety. Needless to say we were all very pleased and the dog had a meal fit for the hero that she was. That dog was simply loyal to the max and she would have given her very life for my wife. The word says that I should be the same and I hope I am.

Ephesians 5:25
Husbands, love your wives, just as Christ loved the church and gave himself up for her

Dan Says:
Real love does not count the cost.

# Moments
## of Ministry

## October 19

My wife does not think that I have the best taste buds in town. She does not always understand that I am not so much for watching calories. If the food was on a pig I love it no matter what you do to it. In fact one of my favorite foods is SPAM it is made for those with discriminating taste. The best way to have spam is to have it fried with eggs, but it is also very good on sandwiches with cheese. Over ninety percent of all spam made is consumed in the Pacific islands. Maybe that is why those islanders tend to be rather large. All I know is this if you had a fried spam pieces and a plate of beans you are almost in culinary heaven. I even have a spam tee shirt and hat, which I proudly wear.

Psalm 22:26
The poor will eat and be satisfied; those who seek the Lord will praise him

Dan Says:
My best is not always your best.

# Moments
## of Ministry

# October 20

I had just come home from boot camp and was unaware that I had acquired some really bad habits. After six weeks with a bunch of men from the Deep South my language was not the best for mixed company. I really was trying to watch what I said but one night was unsuccessful. We were sitting at the dinner table and I suddenly found myself on the floor looking up at the table wondering how I got there. Well it seems as though I asked my mother to pass the @#$%^ bread and my father took offense at the remark and backhanded me. I was deeply sorry and apologized to all, but I did learn that I could control my mouth if I wanted to.

James 3:9
With the tongue we praise our Lord and Father, and with it we curse human beings, who have been made in God's likeness.

Dan Says:
The character of a man shows in his speech.

# Moments of Ministry

# October 21

The church that I was serving at decided to start a drama department and so we began to put on short productions. We got to be pretty good at putting on dramas and soon we would fill the church. Finally the woman in charge of the drama department said we were ready to put on a production at the community playhouse. We did really well and the audiences were giving us good reviews and we were having a great time ourselves. On the last night we were pretty loose about the play and soon we began to make small mistakes. Once I was to talk to a lady in a chair, but she forgot to come on stage. Everyone in the audience must have thought I was crazy. Well I guess they had that right anyway.

Hebrews 12:14
Make every effort to live in peace with everyone and to be holy; without holiness no one will see the Lord.

Dan Says:
Even when you are not there you can be an embarrassment to others.

# Moments of Ministry

# October 22

Coming downstairs from our rooms in the Arab hotel we were all starving. When we went through the "help yourself" food lines everyone got different types of food. I myself like to experiment with foods from different cultures so I had a plate full of food that I did not know what it was. Some was very good and some very bad. Sitting across from me was another pastor who decided to go more American with his food. As we were sitting talking I looked over at the pastor's plate and a bug crawled out from under his pizza but that was not the worst part. Soon as it crawled out from under the pizza it rolled over and died. I almost did also laughing at the look on his face.

Colossians 2:16
Therefore do not let anyone judge you by what you eat or drink, or with regard to a religious festival,

Dan Says:
Eat to live do not live to eat.

# Moments
## of Ministry

# October 23

It was a very large class at Golden Gate Law School and I was one of many students sitting in the auditorium listening to the professor speaking. I had taken the class to help me with my occupation as a police officer. The government had decided that it would be wise to give the police officers higher education and had established grant money so they could attend school. I thought it was a good chance for me to advance in my chosen profession. We were discussing a case that had occurred in San Francisco that had gone to the state supreme court. The professor made a statement that simply was not true and I spoke up and said he was wrong. He said "I am the professor here!" and I replied, "If you look you will see I was the arresting officer in this case". He said to see him after class and when I did he offered to give me a "B" in the class if I never came back. I agreed happily.

Matthew 7:29
...because he taught as one who had authority, and not as their teachers of the law.

Dan Says:
There are experts who teach, but I like experts who do.

# Moments
## of Ministry

# October 24

For the life of me I can't understand why my dog hates my Kindle reader. He has eaten two of them now and I think he has his eyes on the one I have now. I know you think I must be stupid to leave my kindle where he can find it. That is true but being in ministry I sometimes get a call and just get up and go. I wish that there was some way to discourage my dog from his behavior but he is fully aware of how to pull the right strings to get me all riled up. My precious wife always gets him out of the hole by going and getting me another reader. So now he has found her weak spot when he wants her attention he can always get it with one of her shoes. She yells and I laugh and am thankful it was not my property.

Ephesians 4:28
Anyone who has been stealing must steal no longer…

Dan Says:
Temptation is very hard for those with small brains like a dog.

# Moments
## of Ministry

# October 25

Excitement ran through all the squares as I announced that I had discovered an arrowhead in my section. At once the director of the dig came to my square and carefully photographed the arrowhead and had all the measurement taken before he told me to remove it. It was very nice bronze piece in great condition. He began to expound on how this was probably shot here during a war with Egypt during such and such a date. By the time we got back to our headquarters that night we had a whole war depending on that piece. I was very proud to have found it and did not know what to say when we dug a little further we found animal bones, I think somebody shot a goat but that was not the way it came out in the dig report.

2 Timothy 2:15
Do your best to present yourself to God as one approved, a worker who does not need to be ashamed and who correctly handles the word of truth.

Dan Says:
Sometimes truth is subject to translation or circumstances.

# Moments
## of Ministry

# October 26

Never having had a family room in our lives we were not sure how to make use of it. We had bought our first house in the suburbs and it had been remodeled so that there was no longer a garage but a family room. Thinking that if we were to fit in with our neighbors we should make use of this new type of room. We brought in straight-backed chairs and sat looking at the television in our new room. As a family we finally decided that the family room idea was stupid and moved into the living room with the comfortable furniture. This was much better, I finally bought a pool table and we played in the family room. Way better idea for all. Guess what fifty years later we have a pool table in the family room.

1 Peter 1:17
Since you call on a Father who judges each person's work impartially, live out your time as foreigners here in reverent fear.

Dan Says:
The Jones's do not always have it right.

# Moments of Ministry

# October 27

At the church we were having a game night for the men's ministry and it was a lot of fun. Understand this was a man's church and we catered to men who had not been in church before. I was playing cards at one table and was watching one man get more and more angry. He was fairly new to the whole church experience and I could see him getting really flustered. He finally announced to everyone at the table that he had to go outside for a minute and I asked why and he answered "I have to cuss and I do not want to in church". Now that is what I call growth in the Lord and in this man's faith. I said go ahead and to my surprise he did.

Romans 8:27
And he who searches our hearts knows the mind of the Spirit, because the Spirit intercedes for God's people in accordance with the will of God.

Dan Says:
Christian growth is different from man to man; we must not stop it with a critical spirit.

# Moments
## of Ministry

# October 28

I just finished celebrating my seventy sixth birthday and you may wonder why that is significant. Well you see when I was much younger I was sure that I was going to die at age thirty-eight. So I lived my life accordingly I lived hard and fast and just wanted to leave a good-looking corpse. The funny thing about this is that I really did die at the age of thirty-eight and was born again. Now my old body wishes I had not lived so hard those beginning years. But I can tell you for sure that the last thirty-eight have been the absolute best years a man can live. It is such a joy to be able to serve my Lord Jesus and see what He has for me to accomplish next.

2 Corinthians 5:17
Therefore, if anyone is in Christ, the new creation has come: The old has gone, the new is here!

Dan Says:
Life is lived best when you live it for the Lord.

# Moments
## of Ministry

# October 29

Sitting at the Christian event I was next to the man who owned the Christian bookstore. I introduced myself as the pastor of the church I was serving and he gave me a funny look. I asked what the matter was and he said that there had been many from my congregation who had come in asking for a family altar for their home. And when he said he did not have any they demanded that he order one for them. I had been preaching a series on family devotions and had used the phrase family altar. I guess I should have been more specific in my description of family prayer, but in a way I was happy to hear that they were listening and trying to do the right thing.

Romans 12:18
If it is possible, as far as it depends on you, live at peace with everyone.

Dan Says:
Not all illustrations are meant to be taken like they are scripture.

# Moments
## of Ministry

# October 30

The kids came home with a fascinating new toy and I could not wait to try it out. It was a skateboard and it sure looked like fun so I asked if I could try it out. The girls said that the first thing should be checking my balance. I was really disappointed in their attitude about my abilities to ride a stupid board with wheels. They said to at least try on level ground and now I was really going to show them. Off I went down the driveway and soon I was going way faster than I wanted to. I forgot to ask how one stops this thing so I decided to try and jump off. All I remember is the first thing that came in contact with the ground was my belly. I tore a huge hole in my shirt and had a beautiful raspberry scab for several days.

James 1:19
My dear brothers and sisters, take note of this: Everyone should be quick to listen, slow to speak and slow to become angry,

Dan Says:
Some things are best left to the young.

# MOMENTS OF MINISTRY

# October 31

The dinner was perfect all the men in the senior's ministry had done a great job of decorating and making the church auditorium look very romantic. The food was great because we were wise enough to have bought Kentucky fried chicken with all the trimmings. Wanting to do something romantic I decide to ask the men to tell how they proposed to their wife. There were some real romantic stories and some were very funny, but one was the best of all. One gruff old guy when asked how he popped the question replied, "She was so excited that she fell out of bed ". I looked in horror at his wife who just shrugged it off. I guess she was used to him saying things that were embarrassing.

Colossians 1:13
For he has rescued us from the dominion of darkness and brought us into the kingdom of the Son he loves,

Dan Says:
Sometime it is better to listen to the heart and not the words.

# Moments
## of Ministry

# November 1

Walking into Wal-Mart I could not believe it, there were chickens all over the parking lot. We were getting our supplies as we were on our way to the condo we had rented on the island of Kauai. It was our first time there and it seemed odd to me, as I wondered why people did not just catch and eat the chickens. Soon it became apparent that there were chickens everywhere. Someone finally told me that there was a great hurricane and all the chicken coops on the island were destroyed and the birds got loose and then just became wild. The islanders now market shirts and hats featuring the wild chickens.

Zechariah 2:6
"Come! Come! Flee from the land of the north," declares the Lord, "for I have scattered you to the four winds of heaven," declares the Lord.

Dan Says:
Always make the best of the worst.

# Moments of Ministry

# November 2

Another guy with a knife, I hate knives. He was advancing on my partner and myself and I could not get over the fact of how stupid this guy was. We both had our guns out and he did not want to drop the knife. I am scared to death of knives and this nut looked like he really wanted to cut someone. While we were thinking about what to do a man who this guy wanted to rob just sneaked up behind him and hit him over the head with a bottle. The guy went down and was easy to cuff. I thanked the victim and said he was very brave. He said, "Sure as long as his back was turned." I knew exactly how he felt. Those were my feelings exactly.

Romans 2:6
God "will repay each person according to what they have done."

Dan Says:
God will help when you face your fears.

# MOMENTS OF MINISTRY

# November 3

I wanted to grow grapes because there is so much in the Word of God about them. When the vines were planted they grew like crazy and I had a good crop of grapes. Then it came time to trim the vines and I just could not make myself cut them. They had grown on the top of the fence and were several feet long. So the next year I had a beautiful vine that did not have as many clusters of grapes. But the vine was wonderful and grew even longer and the next year it was over twenty-five feet long and had plenty of leaves and looked good, but in that entire vine there were only two clusters of grapes. If the vines are not pruned they can look beautiful, but have no fruit. Kind of like us in our walk with the Lord sometimes He has to prune to make us fruitful for Him.

John 15:1
"I am the true vine, and my Father is the gardener.

Dan Says:
Sometimes the pain is for your own good.

# Moments
## of Ministry

# November 4

When I take people fishing for the first time I get great pleasure in watching them catch fish. It is so exciting when someone actually learns to hunt for a fish, watch him feed and then catch him. Fly-fishing is different. When you fly fish you catch a specific fish that is the one you want. Some times when you are trying to get a fish you pass the fly toward him and another fish will take it. I used to get angry when that happened until I learned a good lesson. I was talking to a man about Jesus in the coffee room at the police department. The officer said he was not interested at this time and left. Then the janitor who was listening asked me if he could accept the Lord even though I was not talking to him. I was so pleased that the Word of God did not go out in vain.

Luke 5:10
Then Jesus said to Simon, "Don't be afraid; from now on you will fish for men."

Dan Says:
You never know who is listening so speak truth with conviction.

# Moments of Ministry

# November 5

The look that passed over our guides face was something to behold. Our senior pastor, Jim was trying to explain to the guide how to hunt in northern Idaho and was telling him how they call in the animal to kill it. Jim was getting very technical and demonstrating how to purse your lips to the call. The little Israeli guide was fascinated by the explanation. And after Jim was through he looked perplexed and said to him. "Jim you call a poor beast in to have sex and when it comes you kill it'. We all laughed and kidded Jim the rest of the trip.

John 16:13
But when he, the Spirit of truth, comes, he will guide you into all the truth.

Dan Says:
When it sounds too good to be true it usually is.

# Moments of Ministry

# November 6

My new wife had written me a letter saying that her dad was very angry with us. I was on the Missouri so I was not too worried about how my Father-in-law felt back in San Francisco. But after looking at the problem from his point of view I could see why he was upset. You see when we got married we had no place to stay so my in laws went away for some time. It was a very nice gesture on their part. My wife and I got to play house and we enjoyed the experience a lot. We entertained guests for dinner and since the only thing that my wife could cook was steak we emptied the freezer of every single steak. He had a good memory and reminded us often of the missing steaks; even so he was a really good guy.

Luke 6:41
Give, and it will be given to you. A good measure, pressed down, shaken together and running over, will be poured into your lap.

Dan Says:
A Christian also shares the good stuff.

# Moments of Ministry

# November 7

He came out of the house with his eyes very wide and appeared to be scared. I had taken my position. There was a car between myself and the suspect who was holding an officer at gunpoint. The suspect told us to back off or he would kill the officer. I knew the officer and he yelled at me "don't do it'. He knew there was no way I was going to let the suspect take him away. I placed my hands on the roof of the car and got a good sight picture on my revolver and waited for the suspect to put his head out to the side to talk. As soon as he did I shot at him and hit him. He fell to the ground and the officer came running at me as angry as could be. He said I almost killed him, but all I did was put a little nick in his ear.

Proverbs 24:11
Rescue those being led away to death; hold back those staggering toward slaughter.

Dan Says:
Trust those that God has put in your life.

# Moments of Ministry

# November 8

The very idea of contact lenses had not been used much. The young officer candidate was taking his vision test for entrance into the police academy. He took off his glasses and was able to read well enough to be admitted to the academy. What they did not realize was the officer had on contact lenses with his glasses. We all found out later, but by then he already had a nickname "Blinky". If you had the opportunity to ride with him you never, never let him drive. He was in several accidents and the department finally gave him a choice quit or desk job. He chose the desk and was very good at dealing with the public when they came into the station. He also had plenty of time to study for promotion and when he retired he was a captain. There is a place for everyone who wanted it bad enough.

Psalm 77:4
You kept my eyes from closing; I was too troubled to speak.

Dan Says:
Success comes to those who refuse to give in to troubles.

# Moments of Ministry

# November 9

Sitting down to eat my cereal in the morning is always a wonderful time because I get to thank God for the food. It is not the first time that the food is prayed over, I grow the berries in my garden and believe me there is a lot of prayer that goes into them. I pray for them when I plant them and I pray for the blossoms and also for the bees to come and do their thing. As they mature I pray that they will be sweet and big. And finally I pray thanks as I harvest them. How great is that process that God has made for the maturing of those berries. It is a good illustration for me to continue in prayer for my family, church and ministry that He has provided for me.

Luke 6:1
One Sabbath Jesus was going through the grain fields, and his disciples began to pick some heads of grain, rub them in their hands and eat the kernels.

Dan Says:
You get the benefit of all He does for you.

# Moments of Ministry

# November 10

When a call for a lost child comes over the air, every policeman in the entire area responds to find the child. It is something to behold as even the guys with gold badges drop everything to help in the search. The radio even is quiet as no one wants to bother the dispatchers as they go through the whole list of questions that have to be answered. There will be no lunch breaks and guys who are supposed to go off duty will stay and work overtime without any thought of compensation. Sometimes there are tears of frustration when the news is bad, but other times when a child is found safe the whole department celebrates. It is not unusual to hear sirens and horns being blown with joy. Also you hear the joy in dispatch as they celebrate also.

Luke 15:32
But we had to celebrate and be glad, because this brother of yours was dead and is alive again; he was lost and is found.'"

Dan Says:
God wants us to be as diligent with His lost children.

# Moments of Ministry

## November 11

When you live in snow country the winters are very beautiful and there is nothing as beautiful as a covering of fresh white snow. Those of us who live in snow country also know that the beautiful white snow had to be removed from walks and drive ways. We learn to get by and one of the most important things is clearing your mailbox for postal deliveries. Believe it or not one of the things you learn to hate is the dreaded snowplow. He comes by and leaves a berm in front of your driveway and mailbox. One time the driver left me a six-foot berm in front and I called and complained. He was going to show me, he came back and made it worse. I live on the same block as our mayor so I went and got him to show him what happened. One phone call and the driver was back to plow the mess away. He wanted me to use a shovel and so was he as far as I was concerned, the mayor agreed and the driver spent some time working to clear the mess and cursing me under his breath.

Romans 13:6
This is also why you pay taxes, for the authorities are God's servants, who give their full time to governing.

Dan Says:
If you abuse authority some day you will pay.

# MOMENTS
## OF MINISTRY

## November 12

In every mystery book that I read about the British Isles the people at some point go to a pub and order a shepherds pie. When we finally got to go out to eat in Ireland I said I wanted a shepherds pie so we found a pub and I ordered it. When you have great expectations they very rarely come to pass. However, this time it was even better than I imagined I enjoyed every bite. I was with my daughter when we had the meal and told her how pleased I was with it. She looked at me and reminded me that being one hundred percent Irish why would that be a surprise to me. I guess she was right because I loved every meal we had in the country. They are so advanced at presenting food in special ways. Where else can you get ice cream on pancakes for breakfast? What a delightful place to eat.

1 John 2:25
And this is what he promised us—eternal life.

Dan Says:
Do not be surprised at the obvious.

# Moments of Ministry

# November 13

My wife and daughter took my grandson to see the nutcracker during the Christmas holidays. As he watched the dancers he made several comments about how flexible the all the people on stage were. He began to get restless after a while and his mother was prepared and gave him something to eat. That seemed to satisfy him for a while and then he started to get bored again and Grandma said how beautiful the costumes were and how nice the sets were and anything else she could think of. When he could stand it no more he asked in a very loud voice "What inning is it?" His comment gave everyone around a good laugh.

Isaiah 52:9
Burst into songs of joy together, you ruins of Jerusalem, for the Lord has comforted his people, he has redeemed Jerusalem.

Dan Says:
Sometimes all that culture is just wasted.

# Moments of Ministry

## November 14

Getting on the plane in Frankfurt, Germany took us quite a while. I was in charge of the luggage we were carrying on the plane. My wife had gone shopping and during the break at the play we were attending in Bavaria she purchased a cuckoo clock. I did not care about the clock, but now it was deemed necessary for my wife to place the clock in her lap all the way to Spokane, Washington. You may be wondering why that should bother me. Well, she did not take it to the bathroom or many other places so I had to babysit a clock, which I was sure, would get busted while in my care. I think it would have been easier to have a baby than the clock. But the joy on the grandkids faces made it all worthwhile when we hung it in our dining room.

Philippians 3:1
Further, my brothers and sisters, rejoice in the Lord!

Dan Says:
There is a time for everything even time.

# MOMENTS
## OF MINISTRY

# November 15

When he called and asked if I would come and bail him out I was sure that he was in jail. That would not be a good thing as he was my assistant Pastor at the church. I could not imagine what he had done to need to be bailed out, and then he said he was at a gas station outside Rathdrum, Idaho. I got into my car and went to the station there he was waiting with the attendant for me to bring money. I asked him if he had forgotten his wallet and he said "no". "Why then did you pump gas if you had no money?" He replied that he had just read in his Bible that God would provide so he just pumped gas. The attendant was not a believer so he just wanted money. I guess God did provide; He sent me.

1 Corinthians 10:9
We should not commit sexual immorality, as some of them did—and in one day twenty-three thousand of them died.

Dan Says:
Do not show faith in doing foolish things.

# Moments
## of Ministry

# November 16

We set up across the street from Fat Dave's Place and had the camera equipment set to record all of his illegal transactions. I had gone to the burglary detail with a plan to photograph all the burglars who were bringing their stolen goods to Fat Dave to sell. They thought it would be all right for a test so we decided to give it a two-week trial. It was tremendously successful as we identified dozens of thieves and got their plate numbers off of their cars. We had also put cameras in the shop where the transactions took place. Some of the photos were very funny, one in particular was a customer who bought a spring and mattress set placed them on the roof of his car, passed the rope through the windows and when he was finished he realized he could not open the doors. It got a great laugh in court. Dave's lawyer looked at the photos and pled guilty. This worked so good they never used it again. Go figure.

Romans 8:20
For the creation was subjected to frustration, not by its own choice,

Dan Says:
It really is true; crooks are stupid for the most part.

# Moments
## of Ministry

# November 17

I spoke to a group of pastors at a dinner and afterward one approached me and asked if I could come to his church for a period of six weeks to help him get a men's ministry up started. I went and was surprised at the church. It was an old established covenant church that was in one of the nicest buildings I ever saw. As I would come into the sanctuary I always had a strange feeling come over me. The church took to the task and really became a force in the neighborhood. But I still couldn't shake the strange feeling I had in that church. I finally looked at the huge painting of Jesus that hung in the church and realized that the model for the painting was an inmate from the jail where I was Chaplain and he was a child molester. I then brought it to the attention of the pastor. He told me that he could not take down the painting because the artist was one of the church's biggest contributors. It was at that point that I was through working there.

Romans 8:29
For those God foreknew he also predestined to be conformed to the image of his Son, that he might be the firstborn among many brothers and sisters.

Dan Says:
You cannot mock God.

# Moments of Ministry

# November 18

There he was in all his glory "Sergeant Sunshine". The police officer that thought smoking dope on the steps of city hall was a good idea. Sergeant Sunshine was sure that if he brought enough attention to the cause of legalized marijuana that the laws would be changed. He was many decades before the laws did change in some liberal states. But for him, he was just considered a fool. He managed to throw away a career as a police officer. He was not fired right away, but there was no one who would work with him, as we did not trust his ability to reason under pressure. He hung around for a while but was eventually shunned even by the people he tried to help. Drugs and alcohol are not the wisest ways to find peace, only Jesus can do that.

>John 14:27
>Peace I leave with you; my peace I give you.

>Dan Says:
>You cannot medicate your problems away.

# Moments of Ministry

# November 19

Pulling up to the old Victorian house on Height Street I wondered if like all these old houses this one was turned into small apartments. A sweet old lady who invited me into the house met me at the door. It was like going back a hundred years. The furniture and paintings as well as everything else were antique. I asked her why she called and she said that she had people trying to break into the carriage house in back. When we went to check it out she showed us the carriage that was owned by John McClaren the man who gave the city Golden Gate Park and many other buildings and parks. I asked if she had an alarm system and she said she did not know if she did. I asked her to call someone I could talk to and she got her attorney on the phone. I told him who I was and asked him if she could afford an alarm system. He replied, "She owns three square blocks of downtown San Francisco". She did get an alarm and I used to stop and have tea with her sometimes. She had wonderful stories of her past; her dad was the first white doctor in the state.

1 Corinthians 11:11
Nevertheless, in the Lord woman is not independent of man, nor is man independent of woman.

Dan Says:
There is living history in our midst, find it and use it.

# Moments of Ministry

# November 20

When he came home from Vietnam, he moved into the mountains of Northern Washington. He had what he used to call a stump ranch and I still do not know what that means. While he was away from people he began to read his Bible and after some time he realized he could not find all the answers to his questions about the word. He showed up at the Bible school with his Bible and a gun in his briefcase. After a while he showed real promise as a student and when he graduated he was number one in his class. We were all sure he would find a church to serve at soon. He did receive a call to candidate at a church. We were all praying for him to get the church, but his wife showed up for the interview wearing a mini skirt and smoking a cigarette. There was no doubt he did not get the church and the last anyone heard of him he is back at his stump ranch.

1 Timothy 6:12
Fight the good fight of the faith. Take hold of the eternal life to which you were called…

Dan Says:
You are never called alone when you are married.

# Moments
## of Ministry

## November 21

How wonderful is this I get to stand ringside at a world heavyweight fight in Kezar Stadium. I was really doing my job and not letting anyone come near the ring for all of the preliminary fights. But, when the time came for the main event there was no way I was not going to watch the fight. I knew that my boss would be really angry if he saw me with my back to the crowd but frankly I was willing to take the chewing out. I was in awe when my hero Rocky came into the ring. He was not as big as I thought he actually was kind of small compared to the guy from England he was fighting. I was faithful to watch the audience when the introductions were made. As soon as the bell rang I turned to watch and I observed the right hand that Rocky threw at the arm of the other fighter and as soon as his hand came away there was a huge bruise and he dropped his hand. The second punch simply knocked him out. Then my job became much harder keeping back the crowd. The boss did not even know that I watched the fight.

Proverbs 20:30
Blows and wounds scrub away evil, and beatings purge the inmost being.

Dan Says:
It is not the size of a man, but the heart of a warrior that makes the difference.

# Moments of Ministry

# November 22

As a Police officer, for fun, we would troll the projects for stolen cars on the nights that were slow. We did this by driving down the street and suddenly turn on our overhead lights and siren. If there were any stolen cars around they would rabbit (take off suddenly) and then the chase would be on. Teenagers who were running scared anyway almost always drove the cars that would run. The chase would frequently go the same route around the parking lots of the projects until they crashed and ran or they would abandon the car. Sometimes as we were chasing these stolen cars people would take pot shots at us from the windows of their homes. Catching the car thieves was rare, but more times than not we were able to recover the cars for their owners.

Luke 5:10
"Don't be afraid; from now on you will fish for men."

Dan Says:
Sin and you will be caught if not here, then there.

# Moments of Ministry

# November 23

The kids were fascinated when I told them there was a real cowboy hero and his name was Hopalong Cassidy. They were sure that I was kidding and made up a name like that. I tried my hardest to convince them that this was really the name of a famous cowboy and he used to have his own television show and even made several movies. They said that no one would name their child Hopalong. This was at a time when the winter Olympics were being contested and Idaho had a world-class skier and her name was Peak A Boo Street. She was really good and the media had a wonderful time reporting on her trials. I wondered how she got the name Peak a Boo and I learned that her parents let her select her own name.

Acts 4:12
Salvation is found in no one else, for there is no other name under heaven given to mankind by which we must be saved."

Dan Says:
Give a child a name they can grow into.

# Moments of Ministry

# November 24

In our legal system, an individual who is incarcerated is allowed to have a religious representative meet with him in private and it is necessary to have someone to check their credentials. I was a Chaplain at the county jail and it was my responsibility to allow religious representatives to meet with inmates. We had very strict standards for these meetings but often found inmates would try to get contraband in religious books and other materials. All of my religious volunteers were in place and things were going smoothly. One day I got on the elevator with the Catholic priest and we both had our communion sets. I said "we are both doing communion" and he replied" I am doing communion you are doing fast food". He laughed when he said it, but I think he believed it.

1 Corinthians 11:28
Everyone ought to examine themselves before they eat of the bread and drink from the cup.

Dan Says:
The Lord's Supper is never a laughing matter.

# Moments of Ministry

# November 25

The church I was helping start a men's ministry wanted to do something special to get the whole congregation involved. This church had a very wealthy congregation so I asked if they wanted to get presents for a whole hotel in the poorest part of town. They readily agreed to take on the project so I went to the small hotel and got together a list of the tenants. I was careful to get the age and sex of each resident and turned over the list to the church. The project went crazy. The gifts that came in were not much good to the residents of the hotel. The gifts ranged from silk stockings to expensive perfumes, to expensive watches for the men and video games for kids who did not have access to a television and other expensive toys that they were afraid to play with. Their hearts were good but the gifts were not suitable for the recipients.

Psalms 112:9
They have freely scattered their gifts to the poor, their righteousness endures forever;

Dan Says:
Use your head to follow your heart.

# MOMENTS OF MINISTRY

# November 26

While I was the occult investigator for the Sheriff in a county across the state line I would attend witches covens when I could find where they were meeting. I would always go in uniform never trying to hide who I was. It was always interesting, to see their reaction when I showed up. My uniform included a clergy color, which seemed to make them jumpy. They finally found a way to get rid of me, every time, they would go sky clad or naked if you prefer. Some people were quite prominent in that county and did not care if I knew or not of their affiliation. One place I always talked to them was in church. After being recognized they seldom came back.

2 Corinthians 6:14
Do not be yoked together with unbelievers. For what do righteousness and wickedness have in common? Or what fellowship can light have with darkness?

Dan Says:
There are those who would flaunt their evil even in church.

# Moments of Ministry

# November 27

There I was painting the cabinets again. I had already painted the dining room table and now it was another coat of paint for the cabinets. I was having a hard time using up all the time I had at home. I used to stop at the bar every night and then come home late. But now I had stopped drinking and I came home every night. The wife and kids were even having a difficult time with me there all the time. I was now a regular Dad and I just expected that now that I was sober everything would be fine. It was hard for me to earn the respect that I had ruined by my behavior while drinking. When I told the kids to do something they would look at my wife to see if they should. I thank God that when they finally realized that I was changed they became the best family that a man could want. It only happened because of Our Lord Jesus Christ.

Psalm 103:3
who forgives all your sins and heals all your diseases,

Dan Says:
Thank God we have a Lord that gives multiple chances for change.

# Moments
## of Ministry

# November 28

While attending Bible College there were classes that were mandatory. One class had a very thick book and was extensive in all the different cases it contained. It was a counseling textbook. We studied many different cases from how to talk to people in the jungle of Africa or how to just listen. I struggled through the class, got a passing grade and went on to finish the other courses and graduated. I became friends with one of my instructors and he had some connections and got me the opportunity to candidate at a small church. After a trial period I was hired and began my work as a pastor. I was happy until one of my elders came into my office and stated that he was molesting his granddaughter. I looked in the counseling manual and there was no help at all. I finally just relied on my police background and turned him over to the local authority. Looking back after all these years I did the right thing.

Matthew 27:4
"I have sinned," he said, "for I have betrayed innocent blood."

Dan Says:
Trust your heart in difficult situations.

# Moments
## of Ministry

# November 29

San Francisco in the old days was a very ethnic city with all the different types of people living together in their own neighborhoods. It was a fun place to grow up and experience the different cultures and foods that were available. The two major ethnic groups were the Irish and the Italians. You could have a pretty good chance of getting a civil service job if the elected mayor was of your group. The chief was always Irish if we had an Irish mayor and it would be the same if the elected official were Italian. It was during the Sixties when things began to change and integration was the big thing and schools were forced to bus students around the city. The end result was that most minorities still lived in the same place and the job situation remained the same. I guess change is inevitable, so we try to get along and do what is best.

Ephesians 3:14-15
For this reason I kneel before the Father, from whom every family in heaven and on earth derives its name.

Dan Says:
Does not matter what ethnic background you are if you are in Christ.

# Moments
## of Ministry

# November 30

When I retired as staff of the church I was serving at, the senior pastor asked me to serve on the elder board. It was a great honor to be asked and I asked if he would give me time to pray about that responsibility. After prayer and consulting with my wife I accepted the position if the congregation would approve of me. I was approved and began to serve on the board. It was very different from being a staff pastor as I soon found out. The Word of God sets out the responsibilities of eldership and I tried to follow them as well as I could. The men I served with were wonderful men of God who took their job very seriously. I found after one term on the board that this was not my calling and resigned my position so I could follow my passion of teaching God's word and assisting young men in their role as new pastors. I feel that job is way more satisfying than that of an overseer.

Titus 2:1
You, however, must teach what is appropriate to sound doctrine.

Dan Says:
Be content in what God called you to do and you will experience joy.

# Moments of Ministry

# December 1

Gaelic football is a wonderful sport that is enjoyed by the Irish for centuries. To explain the game is fairly easy. Each team has eleven players. There is a goal tender that stands between two football goalposts to try to keep the other team from scoring. You can score two ways, three points if you can get it past the goaltender under the bar. One point if you get it between the uprights like a field goal in American football. The uniform is shorts, a jersey, and soccer shoes. Five players are in the front line, three mid field and two in front of the goalie. You can run with the ball, kick it, or pass it forward by hitting with your fist. It is a rather rough and bloody game. It starts with all players, except goalies, standing holding hands in the center of the field. The referee throws the ball over his head to the players and then usually goes and gets a beer. The major foul was taking the Lord's name in vain.

Proverbs 21:23
Those who guard their mouths and their tongues keep themselves from calamity.

Dan Says:
To follow the ways of your ancestors can bring great happiness.

# Moments of Ministry

# December 2

It was a permanent camp we had by the lake with a small trailer and a nice kitchen set up outside the camper that was under cover. We went to the lake to fish and hunt every year several times. Everyone in the camps near us knew that we almost always had some police officer there. They would come when they had trouble and we usually were able to handle it. The game warden also knew we were there and we backed him up on several arrests. We had gone to hunt quail and the season opened Saturday. We arrived on Friday and decided to scout out our favorite spot to hunt and sure enough there were quail everywhere. We could not resist so we just shot enough for dinner. They were on the grill when all of a sudden who should show up but the game warden. Not knowing what to say we said, "Why don't you stay for dinner?" He replied "O.K. I just love those little chickens".

>Acts 27:34
>Now I urge you to take some food. You need it to survive.

>Dan Says:
>What we did was wrong, but it was delicious.

# MOMENTS OF MINISTRY

# December 3

I have always loved to play pool. I started in junior high when I was a pinsetter in a bowling alley. When there were no bowlers I would go to the poolroom and watch the fellows play. If they finished and left some balls on the table I always got to finish the rack. I was privileged to watch some of the really great players who hustled their way through the bay area. When I got to high school instead of class I would go to the park bowl and play pool. I seldom had to pay as I rarely lost any matches. I even have a pool table in my house today. In case you did not know it was originally a game for those of noble birth. Because I have a table I guess that it still is.

Proverbs 17:16
Why should fools have money in hand to buy wisdom, when they are not able to understand it?

Dan Says:
Anything can be done with excellence if you practice, even prayer.

# Moments of Ministry

# December 4

There is a downside to being an old preacher and that is the funerals you do for friends. When I was younger a funeral was mostly for some older person who had finally expired. But as I get older the funerals become more for people of my age and younger. There is a sense of accomplishment when you do a service for someone who is aged. You can usually look at a full life that was full of promise that was fulfilled in their time here. When I do a service I always have a friend come up afterward and ask if I would please do their service. The only time I see all my friends together is at a funeral, I can remember when it used to be parties and weddings and baptisms. But that circle of life sure comes around fast. I read the paper now and am smug because I am older than most that died. I know why my dad used to call the obituaries the Irish scratch sheet.

Revelation 14:13
Then I heard a voice from heaven say, "Write this: Blessed are the dead who die in the Lord from now on."

Dan Says:
One of the exciting things when you are old is waking up.


# Moments of Ministry

# December 5

One more day closer to spring, as I look out the window at the snow falling that seems to be the only thought that keeps me going. The winters in North Idaho are really long and really gray. I managed to find a way to make them longer, I made myself a set of golf clubs this winter they are beautiful. The clubs sit in the garage and every day I have to look at them and imagine myself on the course hitting wonderful shot after shot. It is just not the same as really playing. I think I have played every hole in my mind if only I could play as well as I imagine. I pray for good weather but the answer seems to be the same. One day closer to spring, and one day closer to the opening of the golf course. The good thing is when the time is right; I will certainly be ready to play.

James 3:16
For where you have envy and selfish ambition, there you find disorder and every evil practice.

Dan Says:
I wish I anticipated the return of Christ as much as the return of spring.

# Moments of Ministry

# December 6

Mickey Mouse, a whale, and bunny, that should keep John happy for a few days. When I picked up these stuffed toys I knew they had a short lifespan, as my dog would first smell them then he would take them to his special bed and cuddle with them. Often he would take them for a walk around the house and even in the yard. It was fun to watch him but all of a sudden the toy became some type of enemy and had to be destroyed at once. A viscous attack would follow with parts coming off rapidly and stuffing all over the place. When they were dead enough he would just ignore them and soon they would make the trash. However, the green dragon has lived for months and I find it in his bed lots of time. I cannot figure out why he does what he does. I think God must think the same with us sometimes.

Proverbs 6:15
Therefore disaster will overtake him in an instant; he will suddenly be destroyed—without remedy.

Dan Says:
Destruction can come in an instant with no reason.

# Moments of Ministry

# December 7

He was a hero to my wife when she was a child so when we saw the sign that the Roy Rogers museum was just up the road we had to stop and check it out. Inside was very big and contained tons of memorabilia; the jeep that his side kick drove and his car that had longhorn steer horns on the hood, the door handles were revolvers and the inside was upholstered with cattle skins. Case after case of books and movies and television shows were down every isle. We finally came near the exit and lo and behold there was Trigger his horse a full sized Palomino that was stuffed and also his German Shepherd Dog Bullet. I was getting nervous, as I did not want to come around the corner and find his wife Dale stuffed. Apparently she was still alive.

Genesis 50:26
So Joseph died at the age of a hundred and ten. And after they embalmed him, he was placed in a coffin in Egypt.

Dan Says:
Dead is dead no need to hang around, just go to heaven.

# Moments of Ministry

# December 8

The entire tactical team was standing on the line at the pistol range. We had to qualify more than the regular officers, but we all loved to shoot anyway. The unit commander also used this time to check how we cared for our equipment so we always had an extensive inspection of all our special gear. We were all standing at the line waiting for the range commander to give the commands we were all used to: ready on the right, ready on the left, commence firing. Just as he began to give the commands a sea gull landed on the top of the flagpole. And when the command to fire was given he disappeared in a cloud of feathers. The range master was so mad that we all went on a three-mile run to take some of the playfulness out of us.

1 Samuel 15:22
To obey is better than sacrifice, and to heed is better than the fat of rams.

Dan Says:
Boys will always be boys.

# Moments of Ministry

# December 9

For over thirty years I have been going out on calls that involved tragedy in the lives of those I called on. It was just this year the year that I finally retired that I met a family that absolutely refused to have me pray for them when I gave them the news of the death of their husband and father.

Frankly I was so shocked that I did not know what to say to this wife and teenage daughter. As I stood and looked at them the wife said to me you can leave now. I simply walked away and I guess I looked shocked because two of the first responders came to me and asked if I was all right. I really was not all right but there was nothing I could do except pray for them. I think I was sadder than either of them.

1 Peter 1:24
"All people are like grass, and all their glory is like the flowers of the field;

Dan Says:
I guess if you have no God you have no hell to fear.

# MOMENTS
## OF MINISTRY

# December 10

When we knew far enough in advance that we were going to a demonstration we would always go out to the Mexican district and buy Belly Bombs. We rode in four man cars and were free to respond to any call as long as we kept ourselves ready to respond as a team. The demonstrations were very difficult to respond to. We knew we would have to stand for hours facing a crowd that was hostile. Until we were released to disperse the crown we just stood and took the abuse. Here is where the Belly Bomb came in handy. We all would have a tremendous amount of stomach gas build up and we really enjoyed the opportunity to release it to the crowd. The odor seemed to last for a long time and all thirty-two would just smile as the crowd would gag and try to get out of range.

1 Peter 2:15
For it is God's will that by doing good you should silence the ignorant talk of foolish people.

Dan Says:
The best weapons are sometimes not visible.

# Moments of Ministry

## December 11

I would wait for the paper to arrive so that I could see if my case made the paper. There were always newspaper reporters at headquarters and they often would wait for us to finish our shift and then ask us for reports. When we gave an interview it was sometimes hard to recognize the newspaper account as being your case. It did not take us long to realize that the reporter would sometimes say something that we did not say. We eventually figured out which reporter you wanted to talk to. Once I read an account of a crime and went to work and had people ask me about it. I did not even realize that it was my case. We have an intercessor when we stand before the Lord and I am sure happy that He will tell the truth.

Romans 8:27
And he who searches our hearts knows the mind of the Spirit, because the Spirit intercedes for God's people in accordance with the will of God.

Dan Says:
He will know what we mean no matter how we say it.

# MOMENTS OF MINISTRY

# December 12

There is a song called "Be My Love". Every time I hear that song I have the same reaction. You may be wondering how a romantic son would invoke such memories. Only it is not romance that the song brings back it is lack of sleep. You see in the navy we would get 24-hour passes and we would go to Seattle for some fun. None of us had much money so we would go to an all night movie and try to sleep in the theatre. One time I went and every time I got to sleep they would sing the same song and wake me up. I got so I hated that song. I do not think that I could even survive such a night anymore. But it was an experience I will never forget. Music can cause great reactions in people I guess that is why I love the old hymns.

Psalm 96:1
Sing to the Lord a new song; sing to the Lord, all the earth.

Dan Says:
What was meant to be sweet turned very bitter because of circumstances.

# MOMENTS OF MINISTRY

# December 13

The brand new facility was getting ready to open and the Sheriff had asked if I would do the dedication. After the ceremony ended, it was time to get to work. The new jail was really something to behold. There were no more open cellblocks that the inmates controlled and the corridors that the officers walked and watched from. Now, officers were in the blocks with the inmates and there was a common area for all to enjoy outside of their cells. There were a lot of disputes about territory in the block and also some violence. I went to the jail commander and said I could reduce violence in the institution without any additional cost. He said give it a try and I had the music changed that was piped in from what the guards wanted to light classical and assaults went down forty percent the first month.

Psalm 40:3
He put a new song in my mouth, a hymn of praise to our God.

Dan Says:
Music does soothe the savage beast.

# Moments of Ministry

# December 14

After they filmed the Dirty Harry movie the Hollywood production company was nice enough to leave us the Hogan's Alley pistol range. We all had great fun shooting at the range and really got pretty good at shooting only the bad guys. However, there was one target that was just shot to pieces and that was a photo of the chief of police. He became angry and would not let us shoot for a while but it was worth it. Training to make very quick decisions was in some ways helpful, but we found that a decision that involved the life of an individual sometime should take more time. You cannot always trust your first instinct. However, you could not take all day to make the decision either. You have to train and trust God that you will make the right decision.

Proverbs 28:4
Those who forsake instruction praise the wicked, but those who heed it resist them.

Dan Says:
Think slow, shoot fast.

# Moments of Ministry

# December 15

Sometimes you just cannot go back and recapture the events of your youth. My lovely wife and I got some fish and chips from Ivor's Clam House and boarded the ferry from Seattle to Bremerton. We used to do that when I was stationed in the Navy at Bremerton. We were truly poor in those days and this was such a treat that we loved to take the ferry. Now we were back trying to see if it was the same and it just was not. Now, we could afford the trip and food and it was not the most special thing we could do this month. I can't say I wish that I was poor again, but those memories are truly precious and can't be done again for any amount of money. I guess it wasn't the food or the ride, but the time with someone you truly love and adore.

Song of Songs 4:1
How beautiful you are, my darling! Oh, how beautiful!

Dan Says:
Everything was better way back then. Sometimes getting old really stinks.

# MOMENTS OF MINISTRY

# December 16

Can you believe it? There was a time in, my life where I wanted to gain weight. I did everything possible, I drank protein drinks I ordered two meals when I ate and I snacked on milk shakes almost every day. The weight came on but it was really slow. As part of the TAC squad I had to put in at least eight hours every week in the gym working out. I was required to lift a certain amount of weight and also put time on the mat with other officers. Now, if I am in the same room with a milk shake I gain weight. I guess as our body changes with age we no longer can maintain that physical ability. But we should at least keep our mind in good shape. I attempt to learn something new every day so I use the brain. I also work out with weights three times a week to at least keep what I have left.

Proverbs 14:30
A heart at peace gives life to the body, but envy rots the bones.

Dan Says:
Our body and mind can change, but the love of Christ can never change.

# Moments of Ministry

# December 17

In over fifty years of law enforcement, as an officer and chaplain, I never got used to observing dead bodies. It certainly was part of the job but every time death came to each in different forms. Sometimes it was an older person who had led a full fruitful life; other times a small child who had hardly any life at all. You learn to quit asking why with each death otherwise it would drive you crazy. I know that the Lord has said that there is a time to die and when you have lived with death as much as I have you learn not to fear it at all. Some people think I'm crazy because I want to experience death and don't want to be raptured. The Word says that God will send an angel to get you when you die. The Rapture is going second-class with everyone else.

1 Thessalonians 4:16
For the Lord himself will come down from heaven, with a loud command, with the voice of the archangel and with the trumpet call of God, and the dead in Christ will rise first.

Dan Says:
The thing I want most is to see Jesus; the thing I fear most is to see Jesus.

# Moments
## of Ministry

# December 18

As soon as I saw it I knew it was perfect for my wife, a gold watch and locket combination with a single diamond in the center and it looked so elegant. I purchased it from the antique dealer and took the watch to a jeweler to make sure it was in perfect shape. I was excited to give it to her and began to search for a photo of us that would fit in the watch. I found one and when I cut up the photo it did not fit. Oops! Well I tried again and this time I ruined the photograph completely trying to get it to fit. Now I really began to worry I was so excited to give the gift to her, but now I was worried about ruining all our photos. When she saw the locket she was so excited that she did not even care about what I had done. What a great woman I married she overlooks so much that I do wrong and concentrates on all I try to do right. She is a lot like Jesus in that respect.

1 Corinthians 13:4
Love is patient, love is kind. It does not envy, it does not boast, it is not proud.

Dan Says:
Always look for the good.

# Moments of Ministry

# December 19

I just could not resist, there was a sign on the fence in Israel and it said "no photography" there was no way I could resist so I snapped a picture of the sign. The guide that I had hired almost came unglued at what I had done. I told him I just took the picture of the sign. We were on the Syrian border when I took the photograph. He then said if I were spotted taking pictures there the Army would detain me, as that was where all the listening stations were to keep track of what was happening in Syria. I apologized and told him he could have my film, he said no but did say as leader of the group he expected me to set an example for everyone. It is hard to remember that we are in a country that is in a state of war.

1 Samuel 15:22
To obey is better than sacrifice, and to heed is better than the fat of rams.

Dan Says:
Rebellion is sin. Period.

# Moments
## of Ministry

## December 20

We were on strike again, it seemed that we hardly ever worked; if it rained we could not work and if the sun shined we went on strike. I finally decided to go to work at the shipyard. I got hired and the first day I reported to the crew boss who gave me my assignment. I went into the shop with the plans he gave me and built the project. I then came back and said I finished the job and he said to me that I could not have another job until time was up. I asked what he was trying to say and he showed me a number in a red circle at the top of the plans and said that is how many hours you need to take to finish the project. The number was twenty-four and I finished the job in six. I had to walk around the shipyard with a board on my shoulder till my time was up. I quit I could not work like that.

Romans 14:12
So then, each of us will give an account of ourselves to God.

Dan Says:
Work like you have Jesus for your boss.

# Moments
## of Ministry

# December 21

It occurred to me that practicing putts from fifty feet was kind of dumb. I finally figured it out if you can make every putt within six feet all you have to do on the long ones is to get it that close. There is always a chance you will make a long one once in a while, but making them regularly from a shorter distance is the way to lower your score. As I pondered this in my mind it became obvious to me that the principle should be the same with my walk with God. I should always practice being close to Him and not trying to get His attention every once in a while. Now I want to be a man who is known for his proximity to Jesus. His desire is for us to walk and talk with Him.

Hebrews 6:19
We have this hope as an anchor for the soul, firm and secure.

Dan Says:
You can't get too close to Jesus.

# Moments
## of Ministry

# December 22

How fortunate can a man get? I have a family that is close to each other and close to God. I can come to them any time with a problem and know that the advice I get is Godly. We are very close and spend time together every week and also we vacation together without any problems. The thing I appreciate the most is everyone's desire to help and care for the needs of the other. I watch how my children and their mates care and pray for their families. As a pastor and chaplain for many years I realize this is not the normal way for families today. But, I can always give hope to others by showing them that if Christ is the central figure in the family it can work. I praise Him every day for all He does for my family.

1 Timothy 5:8
Anyone who does not provide for their relatives, and especially for their own household, has denied the faith and is worse than an unbeliever.

Dan Says:
Your family was provided to you by God love His gift.

# Moments of Ministry

# December 23

Praying hard trying to prepare myself for the task I had to perform I approached the door of the apartment. I did not relish the idea of walking up and knocking on the door and tell a man that his wife was just killed in an auto accident. One more quick prayer and I knocked on the door. A man answered and asked what I wanted. I told him that his wife was killed in an auto accident out of state and I was here to notify him and give him information. He looked at me and smiled and said 'Good I am glad that %^$# is dead." He then asked if I would like to join him in having a beer to celebrate. I was not sure if his response was because of shock or some other problem, but he assured me he was as happy as could be. He said he was sad the car was wrecked though.

1 John 2:9
Anyone who claims to be in the light but hates a brother or sister is still in the darkness.

Dan Says:
Hatred is cancer to the soul.

# Moments of Ministry

# December 24

Mike was gone again and this time I was worried. He had been with us for almost a year and was doing really good. He had gotten a job as a landscaper and his boss really like him. This was going to be the same old pattern he would go find someone to drink with and eventually I would find him in a cheap motel someplace and bring him home. He would stay in his darkened room for a couple of days, only getting up when we were asleep. After a few days I would go to his room and make him face the music with us. We would go through all the rules again and he would agree and be good for another period of time. We loved him like a son and the whole family accepted him as a full member, but he could not accept it. He finally crossed the line that would mean he would have to leave and he went to stay with a friend in California. I finally got the news that Mike overdosed and died. The only good thing about that was I knew where to find him, I will see Mike in heaven some day.

Isaiah 30:18
Yet the Lord longs to be gracious to you; therefore he will rise up to show you compassion. For the Lord is a God of justice. Blessed are all who wait for him!

Dan Says:
God can always see the good. He truly forgives without limit.

# Moments
## of Ministry

# December 25

It was our first Christmas and we were away from home living in a little cottage off the base in Bremerton. We were eighteen and nineteen and had no money at all. But my wife bought a small tree and one string of lights. The ornaments were all homemade; we strung popcorn and used the tops of tin cans. She got really creative; the tops of ice cream cups were decorated and made into fine ornaments. We still have them on our tree today. Even though we did not have a lot of money we had each other and fine neighbors and friends to spend the holidays with. The only thing wrong with that first Christmas is that neither my wife nor I had a relationship with Jesus, which is what the holiday is all about. I can say however, that the holiday was full of love and joy with each other.

Matthew 1:23
"The virgin will conceive and give birth to a son, and they will call him Immanuel" (which means "God with us").

Dan Says:
You do not have to have much to have it all.

# Moments
## of Ministry

# December 26

The whole group began to call it the "A.B.C." tour. That stood for another bloody castle or another bloody church. We were traveling all over Europe with a Christian tour and it was a real disappointment for me to see the church that Martin Luther served having a service with about twelve old ladies. We also went to Saint Paul's church in London, the largest protestant church in the world and found the same thing, only a few people attending a service. The buildings were beautiful and all the furnishings and picture windows were fantastic to behold. But there was no life in the church at all. It was simply a dead body that refused to lie down and get buried. The very places that sent missionaries all over the world were now dead themselves and in need of a new birth. I pray that there will be revival in all of those places where God used to be so active.

Proverbs 14:7
Stay away from a fool, for you will not find knowledge on their lips.

Dan Says:
Buildings do not make churches, people do.

# Moments
## of Ministry

# December 27

My brother and I decided to go to the Grunion Run that takes place in Pacifica, California. The Grunion is a type of fish in the Pacific Ocean and every year they run close to shore to lay their eggs and fishermen try to capture them with nets. Someone told my brother about the run and he decided that we should try it. We rented nets and after watching the experienced fishermen around us we attempted to catch fish. You take your net and run into a wave and hope you catch some fish in it. It looked like it was too easy to make a mistake. I ran in and caught about five fish in my net. It was a good thing that I looked to see how my brother was doing, because he was being washed out to sea. He had gotten his feet tangled in the net and fell into the surf. When we got him to shore he said he had enough of net fishing, from now on he would use a pole and line.

Luke 5:9-10
For he and all his companions were astonished at the catch of fish they had taken, and so were James and John, the sons of Zebedee, Simon's partners.

Dan Says:
Sometimes fishing for men is easier.

# Moments of Ministry

# December 28

While I was in jail ministries I had a lot of wonderful volunteers who would give of their time and talents to bring Christ into the facility. All were sent through a screening process and had to have high recommendations from the pastor and board of their church. They would come and give lessons in the Bible and also some practical advice also. One of my female volunteers came into my office one day and gave me a cake she had baked for my family. I was very happy and when I got home we called the family together to share the cake with us. One of my daughters cut the cake and hit something on the inside of it. She carefully removed what was inside a hacksaw blade. We all laughed and enjoyed the cake.

Psalm 126:2
Our mouths were filled with laughter, our tongues with songs of joy.

Dan Says:
A good laugh lightens the soul.

# Moments of Ministry

# December 29

Back in the day of the stockyards in San Francisco there were a group of men who rivaled the longshoremen in their toughness. They would all frequent the same tavern on Third Street and all were hard drinkers. When a fight broke out in that bar we would automatically send several cars to the call. Once when I tried to arrest an individual and he threw me out the door into the street. Then several of us jumped on him at the same time trying to overwhelm him with sheer numbers. He shook all of us off and continued to fight. At last one of the foremen at the yards told him to quit fighting or he would fire him. He stopped and all the workers began to chant "Knocker, knocker, knocker". We asked later and found that the knocker was a man with a sixteen-pound sledgehammer who would hit the beef on the head at the yard killing the steers. No wonder he was so strong and mean.

1 Samuel 1:19
"A gazelle lies slain on your heights, Israel. How the mighty have fallen!

Dan Says:
The mightiest of men can be controlled with the right words.

# Moments of Ministry

# December 30

My family and I were staying at the Banff Springs Hotel in British Columbia. I wanted to stay at the resort hotel so I could play the golf course at a great discount. We had taken the two boys who were living with us at the time and they were properly impressed with everything at the hotel. There were very fancy doormen and the staff treated us very good. Then all of a sudden everything changed dramatically, the doorman changed into a very impressive uniform that made him look like some general. All of the staff was suddenly in different uniforms and the biggest change of all was a red carpet about fifty feet long was laid out the front door. I wondered what was up so I asked at the desk and was advised that royalty was coming to stay at the hotel. I wondered to myself would we do all of that for the Lord if we knew He was coming. I certainly hope so.

Titus 2:13
"...while we wait for the blessed hope - the appearing of the glory of our great God and Savior, Jesus Christ,"

Dan Says:
O What a glorious day that will be when He comes for His own.


# Moments of Ministry

# December 31

Well it is time to say goodbye, I have endeavored to try and do something for my Lord and Savior Jesus Christ. If for any reason you have been touched or brought closer to Him then I have accomplished what I was attempting to do. Thank you for reading this and hopefully you found it helpful or at least amusing. God bless each and every one of you and your family. This book started out as a radio show thirty years ago and turned into a devotional after I retired one more time.

John 19:30
"IT IS FINISHED"

Dan Says:
God can use every part of our lives for some good reason.


# Moments
## of Ministry

Dan Lynch

# Moments
## of Ministry

Dan Lynch

# MOMENTS
## OF MINISTRY

Dan Lynch

# MOMENTS
## OF MINISTRY

Dan Lynch